Dancing
in the Rain

**True Stories: Finding strength to survive
and grace to thrive in the storms of life.**

Zoe M. Hicks

Lighthouse Publishing Company

Lighthouse Press, Inc.
1907 Mercedes Court
Atlanta, GA 30345
Phone: 404 788 1719

First published by Lighthouse Press, Inc. September, 2013

ISBN: 978-1-4675-8100-4-51495
Library of Congress

Printed in the United States of America
Atlanta, Georgia

For

The two Ediths in my life:

My mother,
Edith Stover McFee,
whose sage advice guides me still,
years after her death,

and

My sister,
Edith McFee Lycke,
whose love and encouragement
sustain me in all the challenges
and opportunities that come my way.

I love you both dearly.

Dancing in the Rain

Table of Contents

Introduction and Acknowledgements......................9

Physical Challenges

Chapter One:..19
A Bullet in the Brain and a Trip to Hell
Being Grateful for Every Day and Every Gift

Chapter Two: 31
Surviving a "Terminal" Illness
Learning to Turn Trash into Treasure

Chapter Three:..43
Living with Constant Pain
Choosing a Joyful Attitude

Chapter Four: 51
Loss of an Eye
A Sense of the Presence of God

Chapter Five: 57
The Agony of Physical Abuse
Finding Church and Community Resources to Help

Chapter Six: 65
Coping With Ovarian and Breast Cancer
A Sense of Humor, A Sense of Purpose,
A Sense of the Power of Prayer

Emotional Upheavals

Chapter Seven: 75
A Missing Child
Comfort from the Ministry of Presence

Chapter Eight: 83
The Stigma of Emotional Abuse
Learning to Trust God as Father and Mother

Chapter Nine: 95
Forgiving a Murderer
Healing Through Forgiveness

Chapter Ten: 105
Contemplating Suicide
Music, A Mentor, A Message from God

Chapter Eleven: 115
Parenting Down Syndrome Children
Visualizing God's Presence; Blogging and Journaling

Chapter Twelve: 125
Loneliness and Disabilities
Comfort and Strength from our Animal Friends

General Trauma

Chapter Thirteen: 139
**Confronting Challenge and Controversy -
Paying the Price To Stand By Firming Held
Convictions**
    Sustained by Deep, Moral Convictions

Chapter Fourteen: 151
    Financial Distress
    Learning to Manage Money According to God's Word

Chapter Fifteen: 161
Trapped in an Underground Cavern
    Hope, Helping Others, Prayers of Agreement

Chapter Sixteen: 169
    The Perpetual Caregiver
    Creating a Top Ten List to Deal with Adversity

Chapter Seventeen: 181
    Living in a War Torn Country
    Discovering the Power of Prayer

Chapter Eighteen: 191
    Loss of Health, Wealth and Family
    Blind Faith in the Goodness of God

Endnotes 205

Afterword 218

Introduction and Acknowledgements

*T*hrough the years, having watched friends and family endure trauma, loss, and brokenness of every conceivable kind, and having encountered a few life shattering experiences myself, I've noticed that it helps tremendously to have someone who has endured a similar situation come along beside us to share insights and empathy. This friend, who may be a new friend just to get us through the stressful experience, tells us what helped him or her, and offers insights into what to expect as the dark valley is traversed.

Support groups are one way we help each other through the storms of life. There are support groups for people being treated for every conceivable type of illness, support groups for caregivers, widows and widowers, divorcees, addicts, family members of addicts, adult survivors of sexual abuse, jobless persons, and too many other groups to list, trying to cope with difficult circumstances. In support groups we come together and offer each other our experiences, sharing what helps and what doesn't.

Of course, everything anyone does for us helps. Sharing time over coffee or lunch, writing a note, sending flowers, lifting a prayer - all of these things make the journey less painful and are appreciated - but those who have experienced what we are currently having to endure can help in a way others can't.

Because we all need support when we are caught the storms of life, I wanted to put together a collection of stories written mostly from personal interviews with people who have been in the darkest valleys and found the lights that led them back to normalcy and beyond, to converting the tragedy into a testimony and a ministry. The stories in this book are about ordinary people who dug deep inside of themselves, looking not at their own ability to handle the crisis, but to the God of the Universe, who could and did give them strength and grace to handle one day at a time. Most of the stories are based on personal interviews. Five of them are based on research because I wanted to cover a variety of experiences and I couldn't find people who had lived through some of the situations I wanted to include (such as the story of Madame Chiang Kai-Shek who lived in a war torn country for years).

These brave souls are my heroes and heroines. They have allowed me to tell their stories because they want to help others. Some of them have requested anonymity; some of them have said it was fine for me to use their real names. The chapter end notes will tell the reader whether real or fictional names have been used. Each of these people found his or her own way to deal with the hardship, loss, or trauma he or she experienced, but each leaned on a loving God, trusting Him to provide what was needed. Even as God made each of us different, He helps us according to what He alone knows will best minister and provide for our needs in critical times. For the gardener, He provides new insights into the plants; for the physically abused, He provides a shelter with loving people who tell her the battering is not her fault; for the depressed teenager, He provides a mentor, who tells him things will change; for the professional speaker, He provides a new "line" of speeches based on the experiences with which she is dealing.

Each chapter's title names the difficulty being experienced. Beneath the title, in italics, is a brief description of what that individual found particularly helpful in dealing with his or her trauma.

Storms in our lives are inevitable. Even the Apostle

Paul experienced storms, and God told him it was part of God's plan for his life. When Paul, imprisoned for his outspoken defense of the Jesus revealed to him on the road to Damascus, asked to be tried before Caesar, his request was granted because he was a Roman citizen. The book of Acts, Chapter 27, tells us that to get to Rome, Paul was put aboard a ship with some two hundred and seventy five other persons, including several other prisoners. The ship arrived at a town called Lasea sometime after the Day of Atonement (meaning after the middle of September). Paul advised against proceeding from there to Rome until the spring (storm season was upon them), but the ship's pilot and owner ignored his advice and sailed. As Paul predicted, the ship soon encountered a violent storm. The sailors, fearing for their lives, began throwing the freight overboard, then the ship's tackle and equipment. After several days, with no end of the storm in sight, all hope of being saved was abandoned. An angel appeared to Paul in a dream, telling him not to be afraid, that it was necessary for him to stand before Caesar, and God would save all who were sailing with him. When Paul shared this vision with the men on his ship, they were encouraged, and, at Paul's request, ate for the first time in days. The ship then ran aground, and, under the force of cross currents, broke apart not far from shore. Those who could swim ashore did, and the rest paddled to shore on ship planks. Not one was lost.

Paul and his fellow shipmates had landed on the Island of Malta. Once there, the head of the Island, a man named Publius, welcomed them and showed extraordinary hospitality. Paul learned that his father was sick with recurring dysentery and fever, and went to see him, praying and laying hands on him. The father recovered completely. After Publius' father was healed through Paul's prayers, others on the Island who had diseases came to Paul for healing as well, opening the door for him to pray for many of them. Acts, Chapter 28, says they were cured. Through the "tragedy" of the shipwreck, many sick people were restored to health. We need not feel badly for the rest of the crew, either, because after wintering in Malta, the people there provided another ship and gave the men everything they needed to continue to Rome.

What do we learn from this story? First, as we know, good people (the Apostle Paul is definitely in this category) experience traumatic things. God did not intervene to stop the storm just because Paul was on board the ship. He could have, but that is not the usual way He works. Next, God provided wise counsel to Paul, who shared it with his fellow travelers. In Paul's case, an angel appeared to him to tell him what to do. In most cases, God will send us human "angels" to advise, counsel, and encourage us in the middle of our storms. The individuals in this book are among those human "angels" God sends, and I pray, if you are in the middle of a storm right now, one of them will be God's messenger sent to you. Then, even in the midst of the storm, God protected not only Paul, but everyone who was with him. Yes, they lost the ship and the cargo, but not one life was lost. In the worst part of our trauma, we should expect to see God working, helping, and protecting us. We may even be used, as Paul was, to provide a penumbra of protection for anyone else involved. Finally, God used the shipwreck to get Paul to the Island of Malta to heal many who were sick, and used the Maltese people to provide for the crew as they departed.

Vivian Greene, American author, artist and entrepreneur, said, "Life isn't about waiting for the storm to pass; it's about learning to dance in the rain." The Old Testament prophet, Habakkuk, said it another way, "The Lord God is my strength, my personal bravery and my invincible army; He makes my feet like hinds' feet, and will make me to walk (not to stand still in terror, but to walk) and make (spiritual) progress upon my high places (of trouble, suffering or responsibility)! (Habukkak 3:19) (Amplified version, Holy Bible).

In the storms of life, we either grow up and out or shrivel and sink. With God as our strength and "invincible army" we can come through victoriously, better and stronger for having endured the storm. Inevitably, as the people interviewed for this book will tell you, we learn things we could not have learned in any other way. Their hearts are to use the knowledge and gifts they received in their storms to help you. For several of them, it was very difficult to share. They risked embarrassment, digging up painful memories of the past, and misunderstanding to tell me their stories and allow me to share them. First and foremost in my acknowledgements, I thank them. Without them, this book would not exist. You will see their names (or, for those who preferred to remain anonymous, their fictitious names) in each chapter. Know they did this for you.

Next, I thank Virginia Sowell for the cover of this book and for her incredible patience in working with me on it. Not only is she a talented graphic designer, she is a woman who has the love of Christ in her heart and the patience of Job to put up with picky people like me. My friend of many years, Dr. Bob Siegmann, did the photograph for the back cover. Bob's photography is unsurpassed as far as I'm concerned. I am often moved to tears when I see his work. One of the people interviewed for this book, Georgia Shaffer, an author herself, coached me through the tough phases of the writing process. I am indebted to her for her insight and encouragement. The team at Bennett Graphics, Inc. did the printing and made everything look great on the printed page, and my young friend, Ruth Anne Traynelis, a poet with a gift for writing, edited the endnotes, making sure they were in correct format. My Bible Study group of many years prayed for the interviewees to come in, and my wonderful husband, Charles (aka Smoky) not only prayed for this book, but gave up time with me to let me go to our beach condo to write. Without his cooperation, I couldn't have completed this book. Finally, above all, I thank God, the Holy Spirit. If I couldn't think of the right word to use, I would pray and He showed me; if I was stuck on a story, I prayed and He gave me a new angle; if I needed encouragement, I would tell Him, and He provided. Another one of the people interviewed for this book, Rev. Pat Dunbar, was God's answer to my prayer for encouragement as she asked all the right questions and listened to my heart in order to provide valuable insight and wisdom concerning my writing. This book is a group project, so thanks, everyone! You are all terrific.

All Scripture quotations are from the New International Version of the Bible unless specifically noted, and I thank Zondervan Publishing Company for permission to use them.

Physical Challenges

Chapter One

A Bullet in the Brain and A Trip to Hell

Being Grateful for Every Day and Every Gift

Matthew Botsford was a young, ambitious twenty eight year old married to his high school sweetheart, Nancy, and worked in the family business selling outdoor power equipment. "My life plan was to work hard, save enough money to buy the biggest house on the lake in Bloomfield, Michigan and provide for my family," Matthew told me. That's it. That's what life was all about. Matthew, who had very loose ties to the Lutheran Church, had no personal relationship with God.[1]

In March of 1992, he, his brother, John, and his brother-in-law, Rick,[2] travelled to Atlanta, Ga. for a business convention. On March 21st they ended the day by grabbing a bite to eat at a downtown restaurant, finishing about 11:00 p.m. As they came out of the restaurant, waiting for a cab to pick them up, they heard screams. Out of nowhere, nine millimeter shots from a Uzi machine gun rang all around them. People ran, taking cover any way and every way they could. Restaurant doors were bolted to protect patrons. The shooter stood on the corner of the cracked, concrete sidewalk, high on drugs, looking for cheap thrills with his lethal weapon.

As bullets sprayed into the crowd, Matthew was hit from behind, a bullet piercing the back of his head, knocking him to the ground. Blood poured from the wound, and his brother yelled, "Help! Someone! My brother has been shot! Help! He is dying! Help!"[3]

A restaurant employee ran out to perform CPR on Matthew until an ambulance could get there. Even as the employee and John worked on Matthew, shots rang out again, this time from an SUV the shooters had jumped into, randomly aiming the gun and firing as they drove by. Again, people ran for cover. Rick, Matthew's brother-in-law, pounded on the door to the closest building yelling, "Let us in!" to no avail.

Rick and another man ran for cover, trying to hide between cars. As Rick ran, a bullet hit him, blowing off half his face. He died in surgery that very night.

Meanwhile, back in Michigan, Nancy sensed something was not right. Matthew always called her at the end of the day when he was out of town. On March 21st she did not get a call. The night before, she had acted out of character, and paid all of their bills. "My usual mode of paying bills was to pay on the due date," she said, "But for a reason unknown to me at the time, I sat down and wrote a check for every bill we had."

Nancy's misgivings were confirmed early the morning of March 22nd when Matthew's father called to tell her what had happened. With her heart pounding and her mind saying there must be some mistake, she packed her bag and waited for Matthew's parents to pick her up, go to the airport, and fly to Atlanta. "It seemed like an eternity before we finally arrived at the hospital," said Nancy. "When we got there, John met us and told us Matthew had flat lined three times, but the doctors had been able to bring him back each time."

We were ushered down the corridors of the hospital to the intensive care unit (ICU), where an attendant tried to prepare us for what we would see, "His head is all wrapped up with gauze and swollen. He is in a coma, totally paralyzed and on a respirator. He is critical."[4]

Nancy noticed five people in a room next to the ICU holding red and white coolers, anxiously looking at her. She shuttered, knowing deep inside they were there waiting on her husband's organs, to take them around the world so others would have a chance to live.

As Nancy entered Matthew's room for the first time, she gasped. "He was hooked up to wires and lines and a respirator. His head seemed three times normal size, with his right side swollen even more. His right eye was protruding from under the gauze wrap...;The only way I knew it was Matthew for certain was by his wedding ring. My knees got weak, and my mouth went dry. I stood in shock trying to believe what I was seeing."

Nurses explained to her what they were doing for him as she waited to speak with the neurosurgeon. When the doctor arrived, he told her, with John by her side, how he had taken out damaged brain and skin cells, and that Matthew had already flat lined (died) three times. If Matthew made it through the next night, he said, there was a thirty per cent chance he would live, but he might be paralyzed and even have to be institutionalized.

Nancy emerged from the meeting with the doctor, and one of the organ donor harvester team members shoved a legal document in front of her, asking her to sign to authorize the harvesting of Matthew's organs. "NO!" she screamed, retreating as quickly as she could to Matthew's room.

Nancy's next recollection was walking down a hospital corridor, shaking and trembling, seeing blackness in front of her, leaving her numb and fearful. Suddenly, she felt a firm hand grasp her right shoulder, as if pulling her back from the darkness she felt she was falling into. She turned, but no one was there. Nancy writes, "[I]nstantly, I knew that it was Jesus who touched me. I knew it. Every cell in my body knew Him, and I just could not see Him...I ran back to Matthew's room...looked up and said, "Lord, bring back my husband. Bring back who he is, his heart, his personality. Even if he is in a wheelchair, I promise to stay with him forever."[5]

Nancy had been raised in the Catholic Church, but had not attended since her 16th birthday and says she did not have a personal relationship with God at that point in her life.

As Nancy offered to give up her life in caring for Matthew, pleading to God and telling Him she would never leave him, even if he were an invalid, Matthew experienced a miracle. Before Nancy prayed, in his own words, "Utter darkness enveloped me as if thick, black ink had been poured over my eyes....Reaching out only proved that I was actually contained in some sort of cell.... No walls, floor or ceiling could I discover; yet confined I was.... Evil was present on all sides - an ever-present form of evil....Next came the realization that this thing was eternal in nature....A cell in hell - yes, a cell in hell was where I was being kept.[6]

"Then I was chained - chains on my wrists and ankles. I heard screams, and the stench was horrific, like decaying road kill. A river of red lava moved slowly toward my legs, as I lay there, laid out crucifixion style. The lava enveloped my feet, ankles and legs, burning off my flesh, causing extreme pain. Then, my flesh reformed, and more lava would come toward me.

"A monster like creature came at me with red, nasty

eyes and flesh in its mouth. It went to my back and scratched flesh off while it hurled accusations at me. I saw other monsters screaming.

"Then, from on high, in the topmost right-hand corner of my sight, a massive index finger appeared. It descended towards me until I could see the entire hand, massive, strong, full of life. Surrounding the hand shone brilliant white light. For the first time, I heard an ethereal sound, a symphony of sound and praise.... The hand gently wrapped itself around my whole body... and I began an ascent which felt like an elevator ride, going straight up. Then I heard a commanding voice that sounded like a thunderous clap of lightning, a great wind and white water rapids all rolled together saying, 'It's not your time.'

"In an instant, all the fear was gone. All the blackness lifted...Evil disappeared....It was obvious that my confines and all of its hellish characteristics were subservient to this voice...I knew...that everything was going to be okay."[7]

Sixteen years later, after Matthew had been walking closely with God, even ministering to men who needed to feel the Father's love, God revealed, in a vision, what happened that day when he was pulled out of hell.

First, God showed Matthew that there were legal issues at stake, for without legality, justice could not reign on earth. As Nancy pleaded, "I promise to stay with him forever," a formal petition was handed to Jesus.

Note the sacrifice Nancy, a twenty eight year old bride, was willing to make - exchanging her dreams, her hopes, her desires - all she wanted - for her husband's life. She was willing to lay it all down, even as Jesus laid it all down for us.

In the vision, Matthew saw Jesus taking Nancy's petition to the throne of the Father. Jesus, wearing a full length, dazzling white robe with a gold chord belt, approached the Father, with his "dark, golden brown hair reminiscent of a lion's mane."

"Father," Jesus announced, "We have new evidence that has just come into my hands....You know that according to the law, Matthew must go to hell....It is the law and the grace that we have established from the foundations of the world."

"He did not know You, the slain Lamb, my only Son, upon his death," God responded.

Then, Jesus handed Nancy's petition to God. He reached out to retrieve it, unrolling it and noticing every detail, including Nancy's tears, still glistening on the scroll. After a few moments, God spoke, "Well now, this does shed light on our decision, doesn't it? Now I can legally penetrate satan's realm and retrieve Matthew from his dire confines in hell."[8]

Matthew believes that the marriage covenant, a biblical covenant, created the basis for the legal argument. When Nancy, in her role as wife, made a whole hearted, I don't care what I have to endure, just give me back my husband, argument, Jesus moved into action. Then and only then was God able to act out of His divine mercy and pluck Matthew out of hell. Though Nancy had ignored Jesus all of her adult life, when He touched her in the hospital, she knew Him and addressed "Him as, "Lord."

Matthew stayed in a coma for twenty seven days, but Nancy saw him making progress far more quickly than the doctors predicted. They told her he would be on kidney dialysis for three weeks; he was on it for three days. Finally, he awoke, not understanding where he was or what had happened.

After a few more days at the Atlanta hospital, Matthew was sent back to Michigan to begin the painful, extended rehabilitation process. He weighed ninety five pounds and was cognitively still in what Matthew and Nancy call la-la land.

Matthew came to understand quickly that he would have to adapt to a new body that simply did not do what his old body did. He writes, "If ever I needed grace to get through a situation, it definitely was this situation. After being stripped of everything I deemed valuable and important in my life - job, finances, being the head of the household, husbandly duties, masculinity and all around fixer and jack of all trades - little did I know that I was being set up for success in the kingdom of God."[9]

Therapists of every form and fashion worked with Matthew to get him back to being able to perform basic life tasks - physical therapists, speech therapists, cognitive therapists, and occupational therapists. Though he was told he would never walk again, he finally beat the odds, first standing on his own, then walking with the help of a brace on his left leg. Matthew's right side was not paralyzed (his left was), but, unfortunately, he was left handed, forcing him to have to relearn to write with his right hand.

Matthew admits the various therapeutic modalities, physical and cognitive, were painful. "[I]magine yourself staring at and thinking about nothing else but moving your index finger...and you try so hard to move it that you get out of breath, your face turns red, and your brow becomes moist with perspiration, and the therapist has to remind you to breathe and says, 'Okay, that's enough for now. We'll do more later on.'"[10]

As hard as the physical and cognitive therapies were for Matthew, the experience of being in a wheelchair and then, later, living with a brace on his leg, were equally challenging. "All the times we've been overlooked and passed over because of my handicapped appearance, we've got a lot of reasons to pick up many ugly offenses if not for the saving grace of our Daddy." (Matthew's name for God)[11]

Matthew had to lean hard on God any time someone treated him as an inferior, or worse, as a non person because of his disability. He cites a favorite scripture, "Not by might, nor by power, but by my spirit says the Lord Almighty."[12]

As Matthew slowly regained use of his mind and body, he and Nancy knew it was time to find a church and learn more about the Lord who graciously and miraculously answered Nancy's hospital plea. They moved to Florida where the weather was better for Matthew and started attending a church recommended by a neighbor. When one of the pastors from the church moved to another city to plant a new church, Matthew and Nancy felt led to join him. They began to enroll in leadership courses, and over time, were invited to speak, minister and appear on national television shows. They founded a ministry, Seeds of Love. Someone suggested they write a book, so Matthew and Nancy, after prayer, decided they should share the remarkable experiences they have had to encourage and help others. In 2010, *A Day in Hell - Death to Life to Hope*[13] was published.

Today, the bullet remains in Matthew's brain. To remove it would kill him. Although Matthew is limited in what he can do physically and cognitively, his attitude is amazing, as is Nancy's. Both have learned to accept their "new" lives and even thank God for the doors that shot in the head opened for them. It's the way they came to God as a loving father and Jesus as their Savior. It has put them in demand as speakers and ministers.

Though Matthew has had to endure seemingly endless therapies and innumerable slights by thoughtless people, he maintains an attitude of gratitude for every day and every kindness. Sometimes, when he looks at Nancy, he can't even speak because he gets choked up with tears of gratefulness for what she has done. When he meditates on the sacrifice Jesus made for him, "It tears me up inside, for true gratitude will focus your attention beyond the gift to that of the Giver."

During his rehabilitation years, Matthew found that having gratitude and being thankful resulted in his therapists going the extra mile for him. It seemed to make the whole environment work together for maximum efficiency.

Rather than focus on what he lost, Matthew gives thanks for what he has, like a right hand with which to type. "Gratitude flows from a humble heart," says Matthew, A meek and contrite spirit, teachable in all ways.

"It's easy to see why I'm thankful and grateful for every day I get now after being in hell for a day and comatose for twenty seven days....Thanks be to God for His choice and its immediate and eternal consequences for me."[14]

As if knowing their eternal destinies as children of God were not enough, Matthew and Nancy also know the Father who snatched Matthew from the depths of hell, will also take care of them in any circumstance life throws at them. When they minister, they remind audiences that what God has done for them, He will do for anyone who asks, seeks and knocks.

Chapter Two

Surviving a "Terminal" Illness

Learning to Turn Trash into Treasure

"**I** came to see my 'terminal' cancer as an asset," Georgia Shaffer told me when I asked her if I could interview her for this book. I knew Georgia had dealt with the cancer, which caused her to lose her job as a computer science professor at a state college, and a divorce simultaneously. At the time of her diagnosis, she was raising an active eleven year-old son who loved to swim, and was working on a degree in psychology in her "spare time." She and her husband had separated, and suddenly she learned she had a two percent chance of being alive in ten years.[1]

By the time I met Georgia years later, she coached

professionals, wrote books, and spoke at Christian seminars. So, of course I wanted to know how she did it. She graciously agreed to share her story beginning with step one: Do whatever it takes to survive. For Georgia, this meant a bone marrow transplant, a procedure where the patient's body is bombarded with so much poison (chemotherapy) she is taken to the point of death before the new, healthy marrow is pumped in. Georgia was hospitalized for weeks during the procedure, and at times her temperature spiked to 104 degrees. At one point, she felt so weak she didn't know if she would survive another day. A helplessness she had never known before set in. But then, just as everything seemed lost, her eyes focused on a card tacked to her bulletin board in the hospital. The card bore the familiar "Footprints" poem:

Footprints

One night I dreamed I was walking
along the beach with the Lord.
Many scenes from my life flashed
across the sky. In each scene I
noticed footprints in the sand.
Sometimes there were two sets of footprints,
other times there was one only.
This bothered me because I
noticed during the low periods of
my life, when I was suffering

from anguish, sorrow or defeat,
I could see only one set of footprints.
So I said to the Lord,
"You promised me Lord,
that if I followed you, you would walk
with me always. But I have noticed
that during those trying periods of
my life there has been only one set of
footprints in the sand.
Why, when I needed you most,
have you not been there for me?"
The Lord replied,
"The years when you have seen only one set of footprints,
my child, is when I carried you."
(Author Unknown)

As Georgia looked at the poem in her utterly dependent state, she envisioned Jesus wrapping his arms around her and lifting her from her bed. "I'm not important enough, Lord," she protested, but Jesus, in her vision assured her, "No, you are special too." Georgia says she felt His presence in a real way. "It was palpable", she explained. "From that moment on, I lived the message on the card."

Georgia's circumstances were out of her control. She knew she would have to unlearn her previous behavior – that of a driven professional – and start over. "I had never given myself permission to do what was in my heart. Before the cancer, I would have said my son was my top priority, but in reality it was my job and career. Facing terminal cancer taught me to pray impossible prayers. My situation was hopeless, but I saw that in partnering with God, miracles could happen. All of a sudden, I had plenty of time because I couldn't work. I needed to rebuild my life, and I looked for resources – a book, I thought – that would help me do it. When I found nothing that helped, based on my training in psychology and my personal experience, I decided to write the book I needed to read."

As Georgia rebooted her life, she picked up a hobby that God used to teach her spiritual truths – gardening. During her illness her aunt, who was like a second mother to her, had sent her some seeds to plant morning glories, a climbing plant. She looked at the package of seeds and thought, *I have no place for a climbing plant - no trellis or arch type structure.* She contemplated throwing the seeds away but didn't know what she would tell her aunt. One morning, while throwing coffee grounds out the back door, her eyes lit on the beaten up white aluminum railing on either side of the cement steps. Eureka! She saw lush green flowing vines covering the battered railing. The unattractive, unwanted eyesore, seen in a new light, instantly had new value. Georgia made the analogy – her ugly, unwanted cancer could, as the ugly railing, be her ticket to the life she really wanted – not that of a driven professional, but that of a mom who truly puts her son first, a coach, a professional listener, a writer and a speaker. Georgia notes, "As I would not have chosen that packet of morning glory seeds, I never would have chosen all the difficulties in my life... yet the troubling times transformed me."

Georgia credits God, "He takes the most terrible circumstances and turns them into something positive, although he usually does it one step at a time."

In the rebuilding process, Georgia, a trained psychologist herself, hired a counselor to help her. "You can't counsel yourself," she explains. "You need a disinterested perspective."

In realizing and embracing her opportunity to create a new and better life, Georgia identified the next step as giving herself time to grieve, recognizing her feelings of despair and seeing that they are as debilitating as any physical illness. Again, Georgia drew on her love of plants in seeing that her life needed to become like a dormant field – "seemingly" unproductive for a while.

Georgia says taking time to grieve can take different forms – scheduling grief time (for example, deciding to grieve between 4:00 and 4:30 each day), erasing all but the most necessary appointments from the calendar, or writing down feelings in a journal. She filled up eleven books over five years as she wrote out her frustrations, fears, hopes and dreams. "We must confront our feelings," says Georgia. "This is when healing begins deep in our soul, even as the seed, planted in soil, imperceptibly starts to grow."

Yes, Georgia admits, grief stinks, but so does compost, dead plant material – pine needles, fruit and vegetable scraps, grass clippings, leaves, dead flowers – decomposing. Over time, it breaks down into rich, dark humus which fertilizes plants to promote new growth and beauty. Georgia calls it black gold, remembering how the stinky, slimy mess will aid the living plants to a healthier vibrant life. Another lesson from the garden.

Grief, like winter, says Georgia, only lasts for a season. When we give ourselves time to grieve and let go of what can no longer be, we are ready for new growth – we are ready for spring.

What does spring look like? We must investigate and get the big picture God has for us rather than staying bogged down with day to day activities like laundry, bill paying, cleaning, and chores. There's a little book, pretty well known, called *The Tyranny of the Urgent*[2]. Its message, in a nutshell, is that the things which grab our attention (the ringing phone, the piled up laundry) are not the truly important things, and, if we are not careful, they'll consume all of our time and attention preventing us from doing what is really important. We need to step back, maybe get away for a while, and broaden our perspective in order to determine what God is calling us to do. We may even need to give up dearly held beliefs to make room for new and higher beliefs. I have certainly lived long enough to see myself do about faces on issues I once felt strongly about.

During the period of seeking God for the next step following grief, many ministries are born. For Georgia, her ministry of motivational speaking and writing began during the time of "inactivity" following her treatment. Chuck Colson, who went to prison because of his involvement in the Watergate affair, established Prison Fellowship Ministries upon his release because his heart was broken for the men still behind bars. When Catherine Marshall lost her beloved husband, Peter, a pastor known and loved on both sides of the Atlantic Ocean, she wrote, *A Man Called Peter*[3], later made into a motion picture. The book spawned her career as a best-selling, inspirational author. The Apostle Paul, jailed for two years waiting for his case to come before Caesar, wrote letters to churches he had founded, which later became major parts of the New Testament. But for the cancer, imprisonment, or bereavement, these ministries likely would not have been born.

Georgia's search next led her to appreciate every day she was given and all the things she took for granted. She took up gardening because of her appreciation of the beautiful flowers that caused her to focus on God, not her pain. Learning the secrets of growing them successfully brought passion and joy into her life. "When we're totally helpless in our situation we focus on the moment at hand. We see we can't determine the future so as a last resort we begin to enjoy the present. Then we stumble over a gift – the here and now." Georgia was learning to smell (and grow) the roses.

It's sad that so many of us think rose smelling is a waste of time. God created such a beautiful world with incredible variety in the plant and animal kingdoms. I live in Atlanta, Georgia, a city that comes alive with breathtaking beauty every spring as the azaleas and dogwoods pop open to greet the spring. Red, deep pink, pale pink and white azalea blossoms dot lawns and surround buildings. I marvel at the shades of pink and the hundreds of varieties of azaleas. And that's just one flower.

Perhaps the greatest enjoy the moment experience of any grief or loss is sensing the love, security and comfort of God with us. Rev. Richard Wurmbrand, a Jewish convert who lived and ministered during the Second World War, wrote *Tortured for Christ*[4], describing his experiences in a Romanian prison, where he was sent and tortured for spreading the gospel. He describes in graphic detail some of the atrocities he and his fellow prisoners endured, but also describes the strong sense of the presence of God that filled the dirty, cramped quarters where they were forced to live. Eventually Wurmbrand was released and found his way to southern California where the sunshine, balmy weather and lush vegetation greeted him daily. He wrote that if he could he would go back to that dingy, dark prison and endure the torture because there he had a greater sense of the presence of

God than he had ever had before or since, and that was worth more than every perfect day in sunny California. The light shines most brightly in the darkness.

Georgia next learned to step out into new territory. Although she had four college and graduate school degrees, with highest honors, she had never done well in English or writing. Because she was feeling called to write the book she herself had hoped to find but didn't, she knew she would have to enroll in writing classes and seminars. She took classes and joined writing groups. After years of having her work critiqued by classmates and others in her writing groups, she landed a book contract. It seemed impossible, but it was true. By stepping out into unknown waters and risking failure, Georgia found her true purpose in life – to help and encourage others through her writing and speaking. Her old life was gone, but in its place God brought ministry. People needed her and looked to her for help through their valleys even as she had sought help in hers.

Some years back I taught Bruce Wilkinson's best selling book, *The Prayer of Jabez*[5], to a Sunday school class at our church. The prayer, found in I Chronicles 4:10, asks God, "Oh that you would bless me and enlarge my territory. Let your hand be with me and keep me from harm so that I will be free from pain."

If we pray "enlarge my territory" we are asking for new ministry, and we will, as Georgia experienced, have to make adjustments and learn new things. God's plan for us always involves growth – moving from one degree of glory to another. We're just getting better and better.

The final step for Georgia in her journey through the desert of "terminal illness" was sharing what she had learned. She had been through the valley and slain the dragon. Through the ordeal she had learned many things.

In writing seminars I have attended over the years, I learned a new term, "monomyth" - the hero's (or heroine's) journey, upon which great stories from all cultures are based. Georgia's experience shows us that real life is every bit as dramatic and entertaining as fiction. Her monomyth goes something like this (I'll call it the heroine's journey because we are talking about Georgia):

Act 1 – Something happens that shakes the heroine to the core, making her face an unwanted adversity. The heroine decides to act, and mentors provide her with gifts to help. For Georgia the adversity was cancer. One mentor was her Aunt Cecelia, and the gift of morning glory seeds was representative of what the plants would teach her through the ordeal.

Act 2 – The heroine encounters her ordeal – makes allies and confronts enemies and begins to learn the rules of the new world. For Georgia, the loving Christ to carry her, doctors, friends and plants were allies; cancer and fears were her enemy. At this stage the heroine reaches the edge of the most dangerous part in her journey. Georgia reached this point during her bone marrow transplant when she felt she would no longer live another day. She battled the powerful forces of fear and doubt, and learned she didn't have to fight alone - Jesus would carry her.

Act 3 – The heroine, having slain her dragon, returns to the ordinary world and shares what she has learned. Every heroine is transformed through the experience, and the imbalance which sent the heroine on the journey is mostly corrected and the path made clear. She has changed and the gift received is hers to use.

Georgia shares her treasures through writing and speaking: lessons from the garden, God's felt presence, and how the pain turned into gain – giving her the life she wanted but simply would not give herself permission to live. Georgia's claim that her "terminal" cancer turned out to be an asset now made perfect sense.

We serve a mighty God who works all things together for good for those who love Him and are called according to His purpose. He did it for Georgia. He'll do it for you and for me.

Chapter Three

Living with Constant Pain

Choosing a Joyful Attitude

S ome pain is emotional; some is physical. Julia Carmichael suffers from constant physical pain emanating from degeneration of the spine and herniated discs in her back. The bones in her spine are cushioned by small, spongy discs which act as shock absorbers. When a disc is damaged, it can break open or bulge. Sometimes doctors say it is ruptured, degenerated or herniated.[1]

Julia comes by her problem honestly. Her mother suffered with back problems stemming from herniated discs, returning over and over to the local hospital trying to recover. Her dad was also subjected to the same degenerative disease. "He lived on pain pills, but he was a stoic," says Julia. "We never knew he was in pain most of the time."

Julia herself has struggled with back pain since she was twelve years old. She remembers sleeping on the tile floor from time to time as a pre-teen because it felt better to her back than sleeping on the bed.[2]

As if Julia's genetic disc pool weren't enough of a problem, an accident exacerbated the situation. As a young adult, Julia was working as a flight attendant for a major airline. On one flight, as the plane was making its initial approach into the New Orleans Airport, it hit a clear air turbulence and dropped two hundred feet almost instantly. Julia, standing in the airplane's galley, went up as the plane went down, slamming her head on the plane's ceiling and jamming her neck. As she came down, she slipped and broke her ankle. When the plane landed, the paramedics rushed in to get her and take her to the emergency room, but the doctors focused only on her ankle. No one even thought to x-ray her neck.

As Julia recovered, she again felt the back pain. After being unable to get out of bed for a month, she consulted a chiropractor, who did, in fact, order an x-ray of her neck. After reviewing the film, he told Julia, "Your neck is a mess. There is a lot of damage and misalignment there." The chiropractor did what he could, but the relief was temporary and the pain persisted.

As the pain became unbearable, Julia consulted

an orthopedic surgeon who reviewed her situation and gave her the discouraging news that her condition was "inoperable." Julia's pain was so intense that she couldn't sit in church and limped to her son's college graduation. She would just lie in bed all day because, "It hurt too much to stand."

After Julia's husband, Spencer, retired, they moved to another city. Someone recommended she see Dr. Paul Gephart, an orthopedic surgeon who handled the "hopeless" cases. As Julia scheduled an appointment, she held her breath. How could this doctor help her when others couldn't? Dr. Gephart ran tests and reviewed Julia's medical record. As she sat down with him to get the results, she could hardly believe what she heard. "I think I can help you," he said.

It's hard to imagine that anyone could be ecstatic about undergoing back surgery, but that's exactly how Julia felt. She was willing to do anything to get relief. Dr. Gephart operated, removing three damaged discs and fusing the bones with flexible rods so everything was not so stiff. The initial surgery was followed by two more to treat six additional damaged discs in her spine and two in her neck. Cadaver bones, rods, and screws held Julia's spine together and replaced lost bone mass.

Although the surgeries took care of the excruciating pain, Julia still suffered. She went back to Dr. Gephart and asked, "Now can we talk about the pain?"

Dr. Gephart referred her to an anesthesiologist specializing in pain management, Dr. Lydia Cartwright, who prescribed a combination of pain patches and narcotics. Although Julia says the pain patches she wears "help some", the pain is not "significantly" better. "Dr. Cartwright has been encouraging," says Julia. "Still, I don't want to take too many of the narcotics she gives me to supplement the pain patches. I'm afraid I'll get addicted to them."

Today, Julia continues to cope with pain on a daily basis, spending parts of many days in bed. She loves to have company. To talk to her, you'd never know she lived with pain shadowing her every movement. Her dazzling smile, showing off her beautiful dimples, her gift of humor, and her warm hospitality make me feel as if she's the minister and I'm the one in need every time I see her.

"I don't want to be remembered as the lady with the back problem," says Julia. When I see her, the only indication that she has an issue with her back is the Velcro brace she wears for support.

"So, Julia," I ask, "How can you be so radiant when you're dealing with constant pain?" Julia rattles off rules that she lives by: "Don't pretend you have it all together; turn every day over to God; keep priorities in order," she begins.

As Julia continues, I'm amazed at the wisdom and grace God has given this dear friend. "Choose joy," she says. "Happiness is based on our circumstances; joy is a choice we make regardless of our circumstances.

"The word happiness comes from the same root as the word 'happening', that happiness is based on something happening to us. Happiness is circumstantial. Joy, on the other hand is something which defies circumstances and occurs in spite of difficult situations. Whereas happiness is a feeling, joy is an attitude – a posture. A position. A place. As Paul Sailhamer says, 'Joy is that deep settled confidence that God is in control of every area of my life.'"[3]

Julia goes on to note that pain is inevitable but misery is optional. "God will let you be as miserable as you want to be for as long as you want to be." Julia has a hard and fast rule that all pity parties are limited to forty five minutes. Then, it's so much for misery and back to joy.

Julia's next nugget of wisdom is to find peace inside the pain. "I have prayed for healing more times than I can count," says Julia. "God finally healed me of the need to be healed." Julia found peace within the pain and an acceptance of her situation that allows her to be at peace with herself and with God. "I often thank God for what I don't have," she says. "I don't have cancer, or heart disease, or Lou Gehrig's disease. One of my friends suffers as I do, and she reminds me, 'We're not going to die; it's just a mechanical problem.'"

"Nothing about my situation shortens my life expectancy," Julia says. "My friend is right. I may be the bionic woman and drive the airport security people crazy, but they'd better get over it, because I'm gonna be here for quite a while."

As Julia continues, she shares how she volunteered in a prison ministry and in children's puppet ministries as a young mother. Her vivacious, fun loving personality enabled her to reach otherwise unreachable people. "I thought when Spencer retired I'd have more time to get out and do volunteer work, but now I'm housebound, confined to the bed most days. I've had to learn to focus more on being than doing because I can't do anymore."

We're all pretty well versed in doing, aren't we? Being is something we don't do too well unless we have no choice. Yet, Jesus valued being. In the Gospel story of the two sisters, Mary and Martha, one was doing and one was being: "As Jesus and his disciples were on their way, he came to a village where a woman named Martha opened her home to him. She had a sister called Mary, who sat at the Lord's feet listening to what he said. But Martha was distracted by all the preparations that had to be made. She came to him and asked, 'Lord, don't you care that my sister has left me to do all the work by myself? Tell her to help me!' 'Martha, Martha,' the Lord answered, 'You are worried and upset about many things, but a few things are needed – or indeed only one. Mary has chosen what is better, and it will not be taken away from her.'"[4]

I remember a story I heard about an elderly gentleman whose son came over once a week to help him. The son mowed his grass, trimmed his shrubs, did his grocery shopping, and cleaned his house. One day when the son had finished all the chores, he asked his dad, "Dad, what else can I do for you?"

The dad, with tears in his eyes, said, "Son, all I want you to do is just sit down and be with me."

I can imagine God, pained by our service keeping us too busy to just sit down and be with him. For Julia, most of the "busyness" has been eliminated just because of her physical condition. She realizes her life is less cluttered with more room to be with God – she can be rather than do. Jesus told Martha that what Mary had chosen would not be taken from her, or, in other words, it had eternal value. Being in God's presence, adoring Him, listening, learning, opening our hearts, seeking His will is our first priority. Sadly, we're too easily tempted to substitute good works instead. One pastor expressed it well, "Many people say that humans need diversions to live a healthy, balanced life. I think we've deluded ourselves into believing this because we haven't fully experienced the true joy of a close walk with God. We are created to worship God and enjoy ourselves in that relationship. This relationship is what fulfills us, this relationship is what brings us joy. There's nothing like experiencing the joy from replacing secular activities with spiritual ones."[5]

Julia has come to understand that suffering has meaning in God's Kingdom. She shows me a devotional from one of her favorite devotional books, Jesus Calling,

"Be prepared to suffer for me in my name. All suffering has meaning in my kingdom. Pain and problems are opportunities to demonstrate your trust in me. Bearing your circumstances bravely... is one of the highest forms of praise."[6]

She has also learned that joy is independent of our circumstances, and we can choose it regardless of what we are experiencing. Another great Christian, the Apostle Paul, echoes this truth. Writing to the Church at Philippi from his prison cell as he awaited trial in Rome, not knowing whether he would be condemned to death or set free, he says, "Rejoice in the Lord always – I will say it again: rejoice! I know what it is to be in need, and I know what it is to have plenty. I have learned the secret of being content in any and every situation whether living in plenty or in want. I can do all this through him who gives me strength."[7]

Chapter Four

Loss of An Eye

Sustained by the Presence of God

I first met Victoria Underwood[1] for lunch at Applebee's Restaurant. She is the niece of a good friend, and she had agreed to share her story with me. Victoria looked like she worked in an upscale boutique with her fashionable jeans and black tee. Gorgeous Native American, turquoise jewelry hugged her neck and stylish, horn-rimmed glasses completed the look of someone who might have been in a magazine ad. If I looked closely enough, I could see the outline of tiny screws under the skin of her right eye, where the opthalmic plastic surgeon had been working.

Victoria smiled and we shook hands.

"Thank you for coming," I said, knowing she probably felt

obligated because her aunt was a close friend of mine.

"I'm happy to," she said. "If what I've experienced will help anyone else, I'll grant interviews for the rest of my life."

I could tell she meant it, and suggested we order food before talking about the tragedy that struck her life three years earlier.

I knew Victoria's story from her aunt, but after we had eaten, I asked her to tell me what happened in her own words.

Victoria began by remembering three years back to a gorgeous June day. Her husband, Carson, and two sons, ages 9 and 13, were going to Stone Mountain Park to play golf at the end of the day – at dusk. Victoria, a tennis player, does not play golf and was not planning to go, but Carson really wanted her to come along. They rented two golf carts and had almost finished their round of golf. On the 18th hole, Victoria waited for her guys beside the golf cart under some trees near the point where they were to tee off. Carson stepped up to the tee and swung back and then forward, shanking to the left (normally he shanked to the right). The ball flew off the tee and headed straight toward Victoria's right eye, hitting it directly. She fell face down, pain pulsing through her "like having eighty-two babies at one time with no medication."

Carson, immediately realizing what had happened, yelled, "Get in the cart," and to his son, Barrett, "Call 911 – NOW." While Carson drove the golf cart, Barrett called the paramedics and Victoria's father (her mother was deceased). Victoria, through her pain, prayed for Carson, whom, she said, was prone to feel guilty anyway, and asked God, Will I die?

As they waited at the golf clubhouse about thirty minutes for the paramedics to arrive, Victoria's father and some close friends joined the family group. When the ambulance arrived, they followed it to Gwinnett Medical Center. The emergency room doctor told Carson it was the worst eye accident he had ever seen, and that they would have to go to the Emory Eye Clinic that night so specialists could treat her. Carson walked out of the room into the hallway and sobbed like a baby.

"It took all night to get to Emory," Victoria remembered. "I was seeing eye patches in my mind and knew I would lose my eye."

Victoria was admitted to Emory Hospital where the ophthalmologists began to assess the damage. Although they gave her the devastating news that she would lose her eye, they also told her that the ball had hit her eye head on and any deviation would have killed her. They assured her she would be playing tennis again in three to four weeks, and that, with skilled hands of the opthalmic plastic surgeon and a glass eye, no one would be able to tell she had an artificial eye after the surgeries were completed (she still needed one more surgery to remove the tiny screws under her skin, and I marveled at the skill of surgeons who had almost completed the reconstruction of her face and eye socket).

Victoria was released after two nights in the hospital. While she had had to heal physically, Carson had to heal emotionally. He had been a devoted husband before the accident, but now he wanted to be with Victoria 24/7. In fact, he dropped by Applebee's during my interview with her just to make sure she was holding up through the retelling of the story.

"God sent men to help Carson," she told me. "They told him the truth. And He also provided for the kids." Victoria and Carson also have an older daughter who was not with them at the time of the accident. Each family member had his or her own needs for healing and coping with the tragedy.

Victoria's primary need was to return to her normal life as quickly as possible. Carson and the children needed her, and yet, she herself had significant set-backs, and had to have time to recover. She began to see God's hand in orchestrating her return to her life and leaned on Him in a whole new way. Even before the accident she saw God at work. About two weeks prior to the accident, she had heard Ben Salew, a Christian artist, sing "Built for This." As she reflected on the words to the song, she felt God was asking her, *What are you afraid of? What do you not want to give me?* When she told God she was afraid of pain, she sensed Him telling her to give her pain to Him and not to be afraid because He had equipped her – she had been "built" for "this" and could endure it with His help.

One of the first friends to visit Victoria when she came home was her tennis partner whose words were inspired. She said simply, "Victoria, it's time to register for next season." Ten weeks later, Victoria played in a match with her A level tennis team.

Victoria says God used her family, her church, the "columns" in her life and her own sense of humor to get her through the first year of surgery, adjustments to life with one eye, comforting a distraught husband, and wondering if she would ever look like her old self again.

While she admits there were friends who meant well but whose comments drained her – she called these the "and" people – she calls most of her family and friends "heroes". The exceptions – the "and" people – would tell her about something terrible that happened to them and how the event wreaked havoc in their lives. "My dog died, and I cried every night for a month because he slept with me so I know how you feel."

No you don't know how I feel, Victoria thought. *You have no idea how I feel.*

"Columns," on the other hand, build you up, Victoria said. She talked about people in her life who had been there before the accident and gave comfort and support in any way they could when she needed it. She shared how her aunt and uncle, my friends, had been "columns." Her uncle, she noted, knew exactly where to draw the line between being supportive and taking over.

When Victoria said she needed several "columns" to support her through the rehabilitation phase of recovery, I thought of one of my mother's favorite sayings, "Some friends are good for some things and some friends are good for other things, but over the long haul you need them all."

One friend got Victoria back on the tennis court, many provided meals and helped with the children, some were there to listen and talk, and others, like my friend, her aunt, prayed diligent prayers for Victoria's complete recovery. The family sacrificed, making sure she and her needs were front and center, whatever costs they might have to pay in terms of giving up time or other resources.

Victoria's mother had passed away before the accident, but God beautifully provided friends, aunts, uncles, and others to do what mothers do for their adult children when tragedy strikes. Her church, in fact, bridged the transition back to normalcy, reminding Victoria in hundreds of ways of her faith family who was there collectively every step of the way, doing what Christ taught his disciples to do: Care for the sick and comfort the distraught.

Victoria shares the story of God's care for her and her family. She hopes others going through tough times will be encouraged by her testimony of God's abundant provisions.

Above all, Victoria had a sense of God's presence with her through the dark days and nights of healing – a "quiet knowing" and "peace in my soul" as she describes it. Life without one of her eyes would present an inconvenience – there would be some things she couldn't do or do as well – but she remembers God's promise, "My grace is sufficient for you for my power is made perfect in weakness....For when I am weak, then I am strong."[2]

Chapter Five

The Agony of Physical Abuse

*Finding Church and Community
Resources to Help*

*E*rica Townsend looked at me across the round, oak table in her new apartment that she and two of her three children had rented with the help of the county Women's Resource Center to End Domestic Violence, an organization dedicated to ending domestic violence and helping those who have been victims.

'I'm a Navy veteran," she told me. Erica, whom I guessed to be in her early forties, had handled classified radio information and communication during her tour of duty. Her son, Paul, had been born 27 years earlier while she was stationed in Puerto Rico.[1]

"When I got out of the Navy," she continued, "I settled

down to raise my son. By then, I was divorced and lonely. After a few years of struggling as a single mom, I met James. He called constantly to see where I was and what I was doing. At the time, I didn't consider it harassment. I let my loneliness color my good judgment. Neither my son nor my mother liked him, but despite their warnings, I married him - on Valentine's Day no less. Within a year I had a baby, this time a daughter, Caroline, and another baby a year later, a boy, Jimmy.

My husband abused me verbally, physically and financially. Paul couldn't stand it, and moved out to live with my mom. Even then, he witnessed the constant abuse I received at James' hand. He called me every filthy name in the book in front of my children. I finally divorced him, but that didn't stop the name calling or physical attacks.

As long as he paid child support, he had visitation rights and would humiliate me in every way possible when he picked up Caroline and Jimmy. He even threatened my mom and other family members.

One Sunday when I was at church, James brought the children back to my house early. Someone called the church and one of the ushers came to tell me. My daughter called me on a cell phone I had given her and told me James was threatening to kill me. I called Paul and he told me to call the police and call him back. I got in my car and headed home. En route, my brother called and told me the police had not arrived and James had continued to threaten to kill me. He shook me to the core when he said that Paul, who had gone to the house to protect the little ones, perceived the danger to be so great, he shot James and left. By the time I got there, James was dead and Paul was gone. The police came and taped off the whole area."

The police were looking for Paul and had "shoot on sight" orders if they found him. I prayed for him fervently for two months, but he did not contact me. Finally his girlfriend convinced him to come home and turn himself in. He stood trial and went to jail. I went into deep depression - the deepest pit."

Though Erica's abuser was dead, the end of her abuse came at a higher price than she would ever have agreed to pay - the incarceration of her son. She struggled with how to explain things to her two younger children and wondered if she would ever regain a normal life. A new kind of emotional pain moved in and she felt helpless, not knowing where to turn for help.

Erica's church family, however, had not forgotten her. A couple came to call and listened as she poured out her heart. One of them pulled out a card with the phone number for The Women's Resource Center and handed it to her. Erica, feeling she had nothing to lose at that point, called even though James' death ended the physical violence period of her life. The Women's Resource Center put Erica in touch with a trained counselor who suggested she and her minor children move to the shelter for three months to get their lives back on track. Erica agreed.

At the shelter, Erica and her counsellor mapped out a

career plan, and, as she talked with other women there, her depression began to dissipate. She saw she was not the only person to endure and survive abuse and its ugly consequences. The other women at the shelter ministered to her as much as the counselors.

On a recent visit to the shelter, which can accommodate up to 34 residents, including children of all ages, I marveled at the fully equipped playground and computer lab for the women to use. I spoke with two women, asking how the shelter had helped them.

One of them, Camilla, a tall, black beauty with creamy skin and lightning white teeth, told me the abuse started when her husband began drinking. "I tried to deny it at first," she said, "but it got worse and worse. I wanted to leave but I had nowhere to go. In desperation I called United Way and they gave me a list of places to call. The first time I called the Women's Resource Center, the computer system was down and they told me to call back the next day. It seemed like an eternity before I finally got through. I was terrified - afraid I'd have to leave him and be homeless. When the system was up again, they told me to go to the county jail where a police officer would bring me to the shelter."

"My spirits lifted as soon as I arrived," Camilla said. "Other women helped me see that the abuse I experienced wasn't my fault. The counsellors have helped me get a long term career goal. I'm getting my college degree on line in business management so I can support myself and my two children."

June, another shelter resident, agreed. She showed me her new baby, three days old. I said, "No way. You couldn't have had a baby three days ago. Your tummy is almost flat and you look like you just stepped out of the beauty parlor." I marveled at her neatly braided head of hair and admired the deepest dimples I'd seen in a long time.

"Well," she said, "I did. And I'm glad the baby is here because I couldn't finalize my divorce until she arrived because of child support."

"My husband abused me physically, verbally and emotionally. I left with my three older kids and lived in a van for a while. When that got to be too much, I took the kids to the county Department for Family and Children Services so they could be placed in foster care. I told them I was not able to raise them at that point in my life. It broke my heart but I didn't see any other way. I couldn't take them back to live in the same house with their father and I could only get minimal wage jobs, working at night, at the time. I even lost my job at the hotel where I worked. When I found out I was pregnant again, I almost got an abortion.

"I went back to my husband for one day. He beat me, and that's when I called The Women's Resource Center. The staff here loves, supports and believes in you no matter what. They renewed my faith in God because I nearly lost it. But then, I remembered what He had gotten me through before and saw Him providing again through the kind people at the Center. He is my greatest support and I know He will continue to take care of me."

"At some point," June continued, "I want to minister to other battered women and to single moms. I want to keep a humble spirit, remembering I was there - where they are when I find them. I want to tell them, "You're not the first and you won't be the last.""

After three months at the shelter, Erica moved into her new apartment, which the Women's Resource Center helped her to furnish. Shortly after getting settled, a neighborhood church group, canvassing the area, knocked on her door. "I just happened to be there," said Erica, "and shared briefly bits of my recent journey."

"As I told my story, they said they saw God involved at every point and told me He would go to the other end of the world to rescue one lamb. I, they said, was that one lamb. For the first time since the abuse started, I felt special."

Erica continues to pray for her son, Paul, and for her own healing. She believes prison was God's way of getting Paul's attention and says he recently wrote her a two page letter about how God is talking to him and working in his life.

Erica recently attended a lecture on healing wounded hearts. She learned that only God can heal a deep wound and that healing comes through forgiveness. Christian counselors and support groups can be very instrumental in getting us to the point at which we can release all bitterness and anger. Then we can ask God to forgive the one who hurt us through us.

She now feels her pain has been productive pain and

knows God wants her to be healed so He can use her in Kingdom work. Her new goal is to love God with all of her heart - to be "all in" for the One who came to rescue her.

Chapter Six

Coping With Ovarian and Breast Cancer

A Sense of Humor, A Sense of Purpose,
A Sense of the Power of Prayer

*T*he hospital's quarterly newsletter encapsulated Blackie Scott Neese's approach to "terminal" cancer in a featured piece: "Blackie Scott Adopts a Buoyant Attitude and Active Lifestyle to Confront Cancer."

The article, which came out fourteen years after Blackie was diagnosed with ovarian cancer, followed by breast cancer five years later, outlined the medical procedures Blackie's physicians prescribed, and included sidebars to present alternative courses of treatment. Though the hospital was highlighting Blackie as one of its success stories, every time it quoted her, she talked of her faith and the prayer support of friends at church and in her cancer support group.

Blackie, not by any means the shy, retiring type, writes and speaks all over the country. Although her neighbors had given her up as gone (collecting for a memorial garden named for her while she was undergoing treatment) Blackie kept doing what she had always done.

"I spoke all over the south ... even California, Texas and many other places. It's important to have something to do, something you believe is meaningful. You must have something to look forward to – a goal. I was determined to keep all my appointments and fulfill my speaking commitments. I never cancelled one speech – not ever." Blackie delivered twenty five to thirty speeches during her eight rounds of chemotherapy for ovarian cancer.

When diagnosed with breast cancer five years later, Blackie opted for a mastectomy instead of a lumpectomy because "I still had a hectic speaking engagement scheduled to keep up. I didn't have time to spend six weeks getting daily radiation treatment." In fact, Blackie added a new topic to her repertoire of speeches, "Humor your Tumor – Laugh Your Cancer Into Remission." On a recent cruise where Blackie spoke on a different topic each day, she reports the room was packed to capacity, standing room only, when she shared how her humor helped her overcome ovarian cancer. "Everyone has been affected by cancer in some way," says Blackie. "If not personally, a family member or close friend has been a victim."

Blackie even became a member of the National Cancer

Survivor's Day Foundation speaker's bureau. When she speaks for them, she opens her speeches with, "This is the year to have cancer! Look at all of the developments out there!" She explains, "I do that to take the fear of living with cancer away."

As Blackie shared how she coped with cancer with people around the country, at home she continued to find support through a cancer support group led by the hospital's chaplain and the prayers of her friends at church and beyond. "As a Christian, I believe in prayer. I truly do," she says. She loves to pull out a map of the United States she made, with marks at every point where she knew someone prayed for her during her battle with ovarian cancer. The map is covered with pink highlights. "Isn't that wonderful? Knowing that people care is indescribable ... and you can't get that from the internet."[1]

Blackie refused to give in to her cancer, continuing her speaking engagements and even adding a new "line" in the midst of her ordeal. She had been helping corporate executives with business etiquette and busy women with entertaining on the run. Now she could help others deal with cancer, whether it was they or their family members being treated. She showed them how to lighten their moods and face treatments with a positive attitude.[2]

I once read a story about a physician who treated cancer patients. He described one of his patients, a landscape architect, who seemed to defy all the odds. The doctor watched other patients with the same type of cancer die, while the landscape architect seemed to be a close cousin of the Energizer bunny. Every time this man came in to see the doctor he talked about his purpose. He had to make some new apartment complex or commercial building or park more beautiful. He lived to create beauty and he knew it. The doctor finally concluded that this strong sense of purpose was actually keeping him alive, because strictly from a medical standpoint he should have been long gone.

A recent study reported in the "Health Day Reporter" confirms the doctor's conclusion. Patricia A. Boyle, Ph.D., and her colleagues at the Rush University Medical Center studied 1,238 older adults participating in ongoing research studies at Rush. The participants, with an average age of 78, were all dementia free when the study began. They were asked questions about their purpose in life, rating themselves in different areas meant to measure the tendency to derive meaning from life and to feel progress in achieving goals. The average score was 3.7 out of a possible 5.

When comparing the scores (after adjusting for age, sex, education and race), Dr. Boyle and her assistants found those with a higher sense of purpose had about half the risk of dying during the five year follow-up period as those with a low sense of purpose, even after controlling for such factors as medical conditions and disability.

"What this is saying is, if you find purpose in life, if you find your life is meaningful and if you have goal directed behavior, you are likely to live longer" she said. Boyle believes the new study is one of the first large scale investigations to examine the link between life purpose and longevity.[3]

While a sense of purpose can extend life, Blackie coupled that with the power of prayer, asking everyone she knew to pray for her complete healing. She created a daily reminder to herself of prayer power by putting a map of the United States on poster board and highlighting with bright pink magic marker every town or city where she heard someone was praying for her. She carried the board to church and bragged on her prayer warriors, cementing in her mind the power of agreement in collective prayer.[4]

Larry Dossey, M.D., who has written extensively on the scientific basis of the power of prayer, confirms. Through controlled experiments, he has shown prayer to be as effective as any wonder drug we have. He notes that no drug is effective all the time, nor is prayer always effective to achieve the results intended by the pray-er. Nonetheless, the results of prayer and its healing power can be scientifically proven.[5]

Dossey notes that prayer works whether or not the recipient is near or halfway around the world and whether or not he or she knows the prayers are being offered. In a study by cardiologist Randolph Byrd involving 393 patients in the coronary care unit of San Francisco General Hospital, prayer groups in various parts of the United States were asked to pray for patients. Except for prayer, all the patients received the same high tech therapy. The study was double-blind, meaning neither the patients nor the physicians knew who was being prayed for. Dr. Byrd found the patients who were prayed for did "significantly better" on several outcomes being measured.[6]

Dossey goes on to explain that we don't know why prayer works any more than our most learned physicists can explain the phenomenon known as non-local events. If two subatomic particles that have been in contact are separated, a change in one is duplicated in a change in the other, instantly, and to the same degree, no matter how far apart they are. Intercessory prayer, says Dossey, bears "strong resemblance" to the non-local events studied by physicists.[7]

However, he also acknowledges that the explanation favored by many that prayer works because "God does it" is "as good as any" and "better than most."[8]

While Blackie's speaking engagements gave her a sense of purpose, she also tapped into the power she had seen working in her life for years, actively recruiting friends to pray for her, even as a fundraiser recruits contributions for a cause. Every time someone told her about a church which had added her to its prayer list, she gleefully added a pink dot to her map. She ultimately had pink marks on 23 states and in 3 foreign countries.

Testimony about the power of prayer in the healing process could fill millions of books, but just as important to Blackie, a born extrovert, was the sense of a community of intercessors lifting her up. Knowing so many people, even people she had never met, cared, strengthened her resolve to beat the disease. She sensed an army joining her in the battle and a lifting of the burden to do it all alone.

One of Blackie's friends went with her to every chemo treatment and asked God to preserve her memory. "I lost my sense of smell," Blackie said, "but never my memory."

During one of her speeches, an artist created a picture of an angel with a missing wing and gave it to her. Her talk that day focused on the need we have for each other's love and support – how much we need each other, particularly during the hard times.

Blackie had the picture made into note cards that she sells online. Part of the text on the back reads: "God has made us all angels with only one wing. We must embrace each other in order to fly. My life has been blessed with flocks of one-winged angels, lifting me over many obstacles. You too can fly, but never alone."

Blackie calls the members of her cancer support group angels. "Because of them, at no time did I feel I wasn't going to make it. I have always had hope."

Emotional Upheavals

Chapter Seven

A Missing Child
Comfort from the Ministry of Presence

W e've seen the pictures on milk cartoons, federal forms and public bulletin boards. A child is missing, and an age-accelerated picture of what the child might look like today accompanies the plea for any information that would lead to his or her whereabouts. We shake our heads and maybe offer a silent prayer until it happens to someone we know.

Celia Summers was going about her daily routine in early December over ten years ago when she received a phone call for her son, Jason. When she told the caller that Jason was away at college, he explained that Jason's SUV was parked on a duck-hunting preserve on private property across the state line from Jason's school. The caller had left a note on the windshield the day before asking the owner to remove the unlocked car. When it remained there the next day, the caller opened the glove compartment and found the Summers' phone number on service records.[1]

With one ominous message, the typical winter day for Celia and Ben (her husband) Summers turned into a nightmare. Celia immediately started making calls. First, she called Jason's landlord but couldn't reach her. Then she called the college security department, which sent someone to check his house, but saw no sign of Jason. Security sent out an email to all students advising them of Jason's disappearance and providing a number for them to call if they had any information to provide.

The Summers next contacted the county Sheriff's department and the state police. The following day, authorities launched a grid search of the area where Jason's SUV had been found, and a helicopter search team soon spied a pile of clothing about one hundred yards from the vehicle's location, near a levy adjacent to a bayou. Jason's shoes, socks, pants (wet from the knees down), a dry t-shirt, and wallet with cash and various pieces of identification were folded neatly in a pile. Celia, who said Jason never did anything that neatly in his life, doubted her son had left his clothes in such a perfectly folded manner.

Over the next few days, according to police records, newspaper articles, and memories of those who participated, a search team explored the woods near the levy and sent divers and boaters to navigate the bayou's swollen and racing waters, examining the possibility that Jason had been swept away by currents more dangerous than he realized. Jason's friends flew to the scene to help with the police search, but Celia and Ben, on advice from authorities, stayed at home, hoping to hear from Jason or at least something about him. They halfway expected to get a demand for ransom after several days.

For the week following Jason's disappearance, ground, water and aerial searches were conducted. Two different K-9 teams were brought in, each one picking up and then losing Jason's scent at the same location. After a solid week of searching, officials decided to call off the search, reasoning that they had done everything they could.

Meanwhile, Celia and Ben were just trying to survive, sick with worry. Celia's sister came to stay and fielded calls. Their church held a prayer service and people appeared "out of the woodwork." While Celia and Ben felt their lives were in suspension, they received great support from church friends, colleagues and neighbors who offered the "ministry of presence." A sympathetic hug and simple statements like, "I am with you" or "I'm praying for you" helped, says Celia. Knowing people cared and reached out sustained Ben and Celia through the first turbulent weeks.

By week three Ben and Celia flew to where Jason had been in college and rented a car to drive to where his SUV, then in the state crime lab for analysis, had been found. They saw nothing that would have attracted Jason to that particular location and began to suspect foul play, leading to their decision to hire a private detective to investigate the case.

Weeks passed. Celia and Ben had to make the difficult decision to allow their two daughters, both younger than Jason, to go on a trip to Ecuador.

"We did not want to project our fear onto our daughters," said Celia. "We really couldn't talk about Jason's disappearance as a family because we didn't know what had happened to him, but we didn't want our daughters to think we were afraid something would happen to them."

The Summers' church, of which Ben's family had been charter members, continued to reach out. The choir planted a cherry tree on the church grounds in Jason's honor. Ben liked the idea so much he decided to plant another one beside it. On the day he went, shovel in hand, to dig the hole for the tree, a friend came out and sat with him. He didn't say anything, Ben said. He just sat there, but his presence was comforting and healing, as if he were saying, "I feel your pain and I support you."

Ben, an accomplished cosmetic and reconstructive surgeon, also reports an incident with a colleague who had to contact him on a business matter. "He didn't even acknowledge what we were going through. Not one word. That hurt."

While the presence and comfort of family, friends, their pastor, and their church community provided crucial support for both Celia and Ben, their journeys through the valley of suffering were by no means identical.

On Valentine's Day, after Jason's disappearance in December, Celia was meditating and felt strongly that she received a message from Jason that he was all right. She says she can't explain any more than that, but it was "very helpful" to her. She acknowledges that Jason could be safe in heaven as well as on earth, but just getting the message comforted her.

Ben, with his scientific mind, explains the process in terms of a natural metaphor. "It's like a wave," he says. "Life is going well. Then a swell comes your way and you are taken into the wave and churned up. Your first need is for breath, and you have to get to the top to breathe. But to get there, you have to let go. The grief of our loss was so painful that we tried to avoid facing it, but we found that by letting go and experiencing the grief, the healing began. The waves still come, though not as often, and when they do, I give into them and surf the waves until they get to shore."

Celia says it's easier now, over ten years out, for her to live with the idea that Jason is dead, although she acknowledges lack of closure is a problem. The private detective the Summers' hired supports Celia's belief with his conclusion that Jason was roped into loaning his SUV to a friend of a friend, who turned out to be a drug dealer. When Jason realized what he was being asked to do, he refused, and, according to the investigator's theory, was probably murdered.

Ben notes this is pure speculation on the detective's part

with nothing to back it up. "He never gave us anything in writing," says Ben.

Ben will not give up hope that Jason is alive. "We can live three minutes, without breath; three days without water, three weeks without food, three months without companionship, but only three seconds without hope," he reflects. Ben feels the father is the protector of the family, and he must continue to hope for Jason's benefit.

Celia found a book someone gave her, *Tear Soup*[2], written by two hospice workers, Pat Schwibert and Chuck DeKlyen, to be very helpful. The book tells the story of a fictional grandmother who had suffered a great loss, although it doesn't say what the loss was. The story reminds us that grief is unique to the individual (the tear soup recipe serves one) and that grief is physically and emotionally exhausting and can challenge our assumptions about fairness, life, order, and religious beliefs. The object of grieving, it reminds us, is not to get over the loss or recover from the loss, but to get through the loss. En route, we will discover that grief teaches us new things about life, and our understanding will be deeper. Tear Soup is beautifully illustrated by Taylor Bills, and at a time in life when concentration is difficult, provides mental and emotional comfort food in an easy-to-read format. Helpful tips and resources are included in the appendices.

Ben found *A Broken Heart Still Beats* (Subtitle: If Your Child Dies)[3] by Ann McCracken and Mary Semel comforting. This book, written by two mothers who lost sons and "lost their way," gave sustenance in the aftermath of grief in memories. One mother was a psychiatric social worker; the other, a former journalist. They turned to literature, specifically to writers who had traveled the road they were traveling and brought back "nuggets of gold." They looked for writers who wrestled with words to say something that went beyond or even contradicted easy thinking. As they collected observations that would "take their breaths away," they realized, without intending to, that they had started a book.

The inspiration they received was that others who had suffered the same loss as they had still found the courage to stay productive in this world. They note that Robert Frost, who lost four of his six children, still got up every day and wrote notable poetry.

The authors found consolation in hearing others echoing their despair and anger, and confirming that mourning is, indeed, a solitary business.

Though Ben and Celia have approached the healing process differently, they both find comfort in their community of faith, family and friends. And, they both acknowledge the caring and presence of others helped them through the most difficult part, and that they are more empathetic individuals because of their experience. Ben sums it up, "a broken heart heals open."

Ben and Celia continue to heal, and since Jason's disappearance, something wonderful has happened in their family. A new family member arrived, a beautiful granddaughter, whom they both adore.

Chapter Eight

Surviving Emotional Abuse

Learning to trust God as Father and Mother

Years ago I worked on the battered women's hotline in my city. Women called in who were in danger of being beaten (or worse), and it was my job to get a police officer out to take them to the shelter where they would be safe.

In order to do this, I had to go through extensive training. In training, we learned that emotional abuse is even worse than physical abuse. Physical wounds heal, while emotional wounds often do not. Although we were not expected to handle the emotional issues of the callers, I came to have a deeper appreciation of the scars left by those who make us feel worthless.

Emotional abuse is any behavior designed to control and dominate another through fear, humiliation and/or verbal attacks. It includes constant criticism and put downs, intimidation, refusing to be pleased, and ignoring someone to whom the abuser ought to be attentive (such as a parent ignoring a child).

It wears away at the victim's self confidence, self worth and trust in his or her own perceptions. The victim can lose all sense of personal value.[1]

Three general patterns of abusive behavior include aggressing, denying, and minimizing. Aggressive abuse includes name-calling, blaming, threatening and ordering. These types of behaviors are generally direct and obvious. The abuser assumes a superior position to the victim, attempting to undermine his or her autonomy and equality. Aggressive abuse can also take a more indirect approach, however, in the form of "advising" (i.e., criticizing), analyzing, probing, offering solutions, or questioning another. The underlying tone of the abuser would be "I know best and you don't".[2]

Denying occurs when the abuser attempts to invalidate the victim's perception of his or her world, refusing to acknowledge reality. For example, if the victim were to confront the abuser about an incident of name calling, the abuser might say, "I never said that." It also includes denying feelings or viewpoints of the victim that differ from those of the abuser, refusing to listen or communicate, and withdrawing (sometimes referred to as the silent treatment).[3]

Minimizing occurs when the abuser questions the victim's emotional experience or reaction to an event or exchange. Statements such as "You're blowing this all out of proportion" or "You're too sensitive" are examples. These kinds of statements suggest to the victim that his or her judgment cannot be trusted or that what has been communicated is inconsequential or unimportant. The victim begins to question his or her own judgment, and self esteem suffers.[4]

I heard a radio host interviewing a victim of emotional abuse. The woman, Marilyn Hontz, who had dealt with emotional abuse as a child, had written a book recounting the damage to her soul and spirit. Despite the wounds inflicted, however, with God's help, she said, healing is possible.[5]

Marilyn was a PK (preacher's kid). Her father, though effective in his work, mostly ignored her, his youngest child. Although she had an older sister (twenty years older) and an older brother (eight years older), for all practical purposes, she was an only child, a surprise to her parents toward the end of their child bearing years.

Fortunately, her father was gone from home frequently, so Marilyn coped by putting him out of her mind and focussed on her mother, whom she knew loved her unconditionally. She naturally favored her mother, triggering resentment on the part of her father. If she cried to sit by her mother, her father would respond by washing her mouth out with soap. Once, on a road trip, Marilyn begged to sit with her mom. Her father stopped the car, told her to get out, unloaded her suitcase, set it beside her on the side of the road, and drove off, leaving her there, out in the middle of nowhere, all alone. The little girl was terrified for the few minutes until they came back to pick her up.

Marilyn managed to live a relatively normal life until she was fourteen when her mother, a breast cancer survivor, told her she had to check into the hospital for tests. Marilyn was not concerned because her mom said it was "routine." At that time, hospital rules stipulated all visitors had to be sixteen years of age. When Marilyn's mother did not come home after a week, she asked to be able to go and see her mother notwithstanding the rules. Her father told her her mother would be fine. She just needed some of Grandma's chicken soup, he said.

After two weeks, Marilyn begged to be able to see her mother. Her persistence paid off, and she was finally allowed to visit. What she saw shocked her. After intensive chemotherapy, her mother's fragile body seemed to be more like a living skeleton than a real person. Still, Marilyn did not know how to interpret what she was seeing, especially since her father kept saying her mother was not that sick. When her mother came home, Marilyn thought it was a good sign until her mother requested some private time with her. She gently told her daughter that though she had prayed to be healed, it was not to be. She assured her youngest child that God would be there for her and that she would be able to make it without her mom. Marilyn sobbed and pleaded with her mom not to die.

After her mother's funeral, Marilyn sat on the front porch

of her house, crying. She turned to God, asking Him to help her and be a mother to her. She told God that if He loved her half as much as her mother in heaven, she could keep going.

Within a year, Marilyn's father remarried, and a strange woman moved into the home. Her stepmother, who did not have children of her own, had her own ideas about how things should be run, beginning with no dogs. Marilyn was forced to get rid of her beloved Chihuahua, which had been a real comfort to her in her loss. The stepmother did not want to hear about Marilyn's mother, and would remind Marilyn that she was in charge now if Marilyn mentioned anything that her mom had loved or anyone who loved her mom.

Marilyn's father and stepmother never came to school events at Marilyn's school, and even told her they could not attend her high school graduation. God, however, was busy answering Marilyn's prayer that He be a mother to her. Her loving older sister and friends encouraged her to continue with her education and go to a local college. After graduation, she lived at home and worked during the summer to save money for her first year of college. She enrolled as a college freshman, excited, as the rest of her classmates, to be starting a new chapter in her life, even without any support from her parents.

On her nineteenth birthday she did not get so much as a card from her father and stepmother. Marilyn was used to being ignored, but when her father called two months after her nineteenth birthday and told her he was done and that she could not come home again, she pleaded, reminding him she needed a place to live in the summer while she worked to save money for next year's tuition. Her father simply repeated what he had said, telling her again there was no room for her in his home.

Marilyn, devastated, called her big sister, pouring out her heart and asking her why she couldn't please their father.

Big Sis knew what to do. First, she lovingly told Marilyn she had to find a way to forgive their dad and even honor him, or else she would become bitter and the unforgiveness would hurt her. Then, she began putting out feelers, seeing if one of her well heeled friends might be able to help her little sister.

The semester was coming to a close, and Marilyn did not know where she was going to live during the summer. When one of her friends at school came in and asked her to go on a mission trip to Israel, Marilyn wanted to go but told her there was no way she could afford it. She had no money for a mission trip, and she needed to work to save money for tuition for the next school year. Of course, Marilyn did not have a place to live while she would be working in the summer, so she wondered if she would even be able to finish her college education.

The trip provided rest and relaxation Marilyn desperately needed with a loving couple who thoroughly enjoyed being with her. When they put her on the plane to go back to college, they told Marilyn they understood she wanted to go to Israel for the summer and that they had written out a check for the entire amount of the trip. Go, they said, and have a great time. Marilyn couldn't believe that anyone could love her enough to pay for her to go to Israel.

Once she arrived in Israel, she realized her sandals were coming apart and prayed for a new pair, not knowing where the money would come from. She hadn't mentioned the need to anyone, but the next morning at breakfast, one of the adult chaperones came up to her privately and said, "God told me you needed a new pair of sandals. You need to go into Jerusalem and buy them. Here's the money." Mother God had provided.

While Marilyn had a wonderful time on the summer mission trip, she had saved no money for college. When it was time to register for her second year, she stood in line, praying, "Here I am, but I have no money." Almost as soon as she prayed her need, one of the financial officers of the college came running up to her and told her they had just discovered her mother's Social Security was available to her and that it was retroactive, which would provide money for the entire semester. Furthermore, he said, she was eligible for a State grant that she wouldn't even have to repay. Marilyn breathed a prayer of thanks to a loving God who once again had met her need.

Shortly after Marilyn enrolled for her second year at college, she met a fellow student, Paul, who seemed to be a kindred soul. They started dating, and Marilyn felt she finally had someone with whom she could share her deepest feelings. In what would prove to be a bitter-sweet experience, Marilyn was chosen homecoming queen for the college homecoming weekend. The college notified her father and stepmother and invited them to the festivities, but characteristically, they declined, because they had other, more important items on their agendas.

Paul escorted Marilyn onto the podium where she was crowned. Coming down the steps, she looked at him and asked him, "Why, why didn't my parents come?" Paul put his arm around her and said gently, "I just don't know."

After the ceremonies, Paul took Marilyn home to meet his parents, and she shared her disappointment with them. They listened sympathetically, and then told her she could come to them anytime, and they would be her surrogate parents. They lived up to their prescient promise because before graduation, Marilyn and Paul were engaged.

Marilyn had no idea how she could afford a wedding, but the same loving couple who had paid for her to go to Israel came to her and told her they would pay for her wedding. She could have anything she wished, they said, a fairy tale wedding if she wanted it. Five hundred people came to see Marilyn and Paul exchange vows.

As Marilyn settled in to her new life as Paul's wife, she marveled that he treated her with such love and respect. She didn't understand how he could possibly love her as much as he did because she had never felt loved by her biological father. Paul had a call on his life to go into the ministry, so Marilyn started reading the Bible and praying, trying to see if maybe God would speak to her from the ancient scriptures.

One day, as she was reading from the book of Nehemiah, she noticed Nehemiah telling God about all the things he was doing for the Israelites while he was rebuilding the wall around Jerusalem. Marilyn believed that Nehemiah was seeking affirmation from God. Suddenly, she felt God speaking to her from the story, telling her she herself had long sought the affirmation of an earthly father, which she had never received, but that He, her heavenly father, would affirm her, if she would but turn to Him. Marilyn began to feel a desire to forgive her father and release the bitterness in her spirit. She felt a sweet compassion envelop her and take the sting out of every hurt, every ignoring of her important life events, and every pain he had inflicted upon her.

When her father called a few years into her marriage and said he would like to come and visit, Marilyn agreed. Although her father had not changed, she knew she had changed completely. His coldness, aloofness, and unemotional interaction with her no longer bothered her in the least. When he called her from home after his week-long visit, he told her that the time he shared with her was the best time he had ever spent with her. And then, much to Marilyn's surprise, he said something he had never said before, "I love you." He could barely get the words out of his mouth, but he said it. Marilyn's mouth fell open in amazement.

Not long after the visit, her father had a stroke and had to go into a nursing home. As Marilyn went to visit him, he shared stories from his past with her that he had never told her before, which included physical abuse and bullying he suffered at the hands of an older brother after his father had died when he was nine years old. Marilyn began to see the emotional scars he had carried his whole life, not knowing how to get the help he needed to deal with them. Those scars would have been passed to Marilyn had she not been able to forgive her dad through prayer and leaning on the eternal Parent who loved her as both mother and father.

On one visit to his nursing home not long before he passed away, her dad told her he had been wrong. Although he had been successful in ministry, starting churches and winning many souls to Jesus Christ, he lost his family. Marilyn ached for him.

After her dad died, Marilyn's stepmother called her and asked her to please come over to the house. She, too, told Marilyn how sorry she was for treating her so poorly after she married Marilyn's dad. She then gave Marilyn precious possessions that had belonged to her mother - the treasures Marilyn never thought she would own. Marilyn saw the power of her forgiveness working in this insecure woman's heart as well.

Marilyn realized that but for the miracles she had prayed for - divine forgiveness working in and through her to these two people who had so crushed her spirit - she would have been just like them. Her children would have carried the scars of emotional abuse as well. Because Marilyn had broken the cycle, they didn't have to. Marilyn's legacy to her children includes the emotional security of unconditional love and acceptance. It's something many of us take for granted, but for those who grew up in a home where emotional abuse existed, it's a gift recognized as one of tremendous significance.

Marilyn heard God's voice by getting into His Word. As she read and prayed back to God what she saw in the Word, He spoke to her. Through these loving communications, she found the answer to the prayer she prayed the day her mother died, asking God to love her half as much as her mother did. God showed his daughter He loved her even more than a father and mother combined, providing for her every need, and protecting her from the long term effects of emotional abuse.

Chapter Nine

Forgiving A Murderer
Finding Healing Through Forgiveness

I first met the Reverend Pat Dunbar at a spiritual retreat where she was one of the speakers and I, a pilgrim. I sat at my assigned place at lunch and there she was, sitting beside me.

She didn't fit the stereotypical image of a theological scholar. I laughed as she told me about her love of motorcycles and confided that she sported a tattoo (though it was not visible). I left the table thinking, What a 'with it' preacher. I would feel comfortable telling her anything.

Later at the retreat Rev. Pat shared with the entire group as one of the main speakers. Most of her story centered around the loss of her teenage son to cancer, but she also endured another tragedy – the murder of a beloved younger brother, which involved years of courtroom trials and is not fully concluded as of this writing.

Pat is the oldest of five children. Her brother, Mark Schwebes, was fourth born. Although they were not closest in age, they were the most alike in temperament. "He was the one of my siblings that I was counting on to help take care of our parents in their old age," said Pat.[1]

Mark served as the band director at Riverdale High School in Fort Myers, Florida. On April 30, 1996 around 9:30 p.m. he arrived at the school to find a gang of young men attempting to vandalize the school auditorium. They had stolen staplers, canned goods and a fire extinguisher, preparing to break in. Schwebes seized the stolen items and told the gang he was going to report them to the police the next day. He then left to go to have dinner with a friend.[2]

One of the gang members, Christopher Black, declared to the others that, "Schwebes has got to die," to which another member, Kevin Foster, replied that if Black couldn't do it, he would.

Four of the young men, Black, Foster, Peter Magnotti and Derek Shields obtained Schwebes' address and phone number from information, called his home phone, and confirmed his voice on the answering machine. They then set out to commit murder. They sequestered ski masks, gloves and a stolen license plate. Foster went home to get his shotgun.

When they arrived at Schwebes' home late that evening, Foster, the gang leader, ordered Shields to knock on the door because Shields had been in Schwebes' jazz band. When Schwebes opened the door, at 11:30 p.m., Foster immediately stepped between Shields and Schwebes and shot Schwebes twice – once in the face and once in the pelvis. Mark died immediately.

When Pat's father called her to tell her they had lost Mark, Pat asked if it had been a car wreck. As she learned he had been murdered, Pat, shocked and overwhelmed with disbelief, whispered, "God, use this for your glory."

Because her parents were older, Pat, as the oldest child, became the face of the family in the murder trial. Mark had not married, so his family of origin was the only family he had. As the family spokeswoman, Pat worked with the district attorney's office in helping to make critical decisions concerning the trial and plea bargain agreements with the defendants. Three of the defendants, Black, Magnotti and Shields, plea bargained in exchange for their testimony. Black and Shields are serving life sentences without parole; Magnotti is serving a thirty two year term (one year for each of the thirty two years Mark lived, says Pat). Only Kevin Foster stood trial for first-degree murder, was convicted, and ultimately sentenced to death. Pat and her family told the district attorney they were willing to plea bargain with Foster (life without parole), but he turned their offer down.

Through the trial and appellate process, Pat has been to court twelve times to date. Foster is still appealing his death sentence.

During one of these court appearances she writes on her

blog (blogging as the Barefoot Preacher): "This week I'm hanging out on a hard wooden bench in a courtroom on the 8th Floor of the Judicial Building in Fort Myers. I am here to give a personal reminder of the man I knew as my brother and friend, Mark Schwebes. Maybe it is better said in this way – I'm here to represent Mark's humanity to the court and to the public. Oftentimes it seems that over time and with the legalese, the victim is reduced to another name on another piece of paper. Their voice can no longer be heard, and the pictures have faded with time. So, here I am, hopeful that people will see the victim as well as the accused.

As for the accused, I hope that people can look at his humanity also ..."[3]

During the lengthy ordeal of Foster's trial, followed by his sentencing and then the appeals, one after another, Pat was serving local congregations as a pastor. She did not share her own personal struggles with them. People expect their pastor to be there for them, she says, to help them solve their problems. In a sense, the pastor is the only one who has no one within the congregation to whom she can turn. Yet, she must minister to everyone else, burying her own emotional trauma as she digs deep within to find strength to comfort and encourage her flock.

Initially, Pat found herself angry. Yes, she had asked God to use her brother's murder for His glory, but she couldn't get beyond her own feelings of anger and bitterness. After the initial period of grieving, her anger was directed at her brother. *Why did you open the door at 11:30 at night to someone you barely knew? What were you thinking?* she asked Mark, not knowing if he could hear her or not. Then her anger turned to the young men who committed the crime, particularly Kevin Foster, who pulled the trigger.

She became more and more bitter, reflecting on the consequences of Mark's death for her family. Her elderly parents were deprived of a loyal, loving son. She personally lost the brother she was counting on to help her take care of them, not to mention a soul mate sibling with whom she enjoyed sharing music, family news and life.

Pat also became fearful, and projected that fear on to her children. She didn't want to go anywhere or let them go anywhere. It was as if she thought Kevin Foster would order gang members to seek them out from his jail cell, just because of their relationship with Mark.

Finally, Pat woke up. She saw that her anger, fear and unforgiveness were consuming her life and destroying her relationships with her family and friends. She couldn't talk with her friends without getting upset and realized she had to move on. She made the decision that she would no longer cater to these negative emotions, and she told herself, I am not going to be a victim.

Even before the sentencing phase of Kevin Foster's trial, Pat knew she had to forgive him to get beyond her victim mentality. She had asked to be able to speak to him, but he refused, so that door was closed. She hoped that he was sorry for what he had done, but as she came to realize, from her standpoint, it didn't matter if he was sorry or not. Her forgiveness of him did not depend on his repentance.

"Forgiveness is not an emotional response," says Pat. "It is a conscious, intelligent decision. We cannot let our emotions control us."

In learning to forgive, Pat had to take her own advice – wisdom she had shared with her congregations: focus on God and His ability. She told her current congregation in her inaugural sermon: "Christ works by taking a group of people – not many that are all too intelligent, none that are too powerful and capable, not many who are wealthy or prosperous – and uses them to show what a great, wise, powerful, capable God can do ... It's not about brilliant people. It's about a God who loves to create something out of nothing."[4]

As she stepped out, having willed to forgive her brother's murderer, she began to share her testimony. Every time she discovered God's grace as she attended additional court hearings, she recognized it, and thanked Him. She saw forgiveness as a process, but she also saw herself making progress. As she moved down the path, she began to feel compassion for Kevin Foster's family and then, even for Kevin himself. She was gradually releasing the power and control he had over her life.

When Kevin's cousin surprised Pat by posting on her blog, apologizing on behalf of the family for what he had done, and saying she was appalled by his behavior, Pat blogged: "Please know that you and your family have my prayers. You are right. My brother Mark was a wonderful man and loved very deeply by those who knew him. He is missed so very much from our lives, but we know that we will be with him again one day through Christ. I am sorry that this is the way that we have to connect with each other. I'm sorry for the grief and pain that you are also going through and that you carry those feelings stemming from Kevin's behavior. Thank you for sharing your comment. You have touched my heart and spirit in a way that cannot be explained and have helped me to move another step towards healing. Please stay in touch."

I have a friend who says forgiveness is a gift you give yourself. How true. When we choose to forgive, regardless of whether or not the offender asks, and regardless of whether or not the offender is sorry, we give ourselves permission to move on. No longer are we mired down with a need to get revenge; no longer do we allow the hurt and bitter feelings to control us; no longer are we the victim. We have taken control and become the victor. We can't control what happened, but we can control our response.

All of us have been hurt by people. Some hurts are minor; some are not. Some of us experienced betrayal at the hand of someone close, just as Jesus experienced betrayal by one of the twelve disciples. If the hurt is deep, I have found that the only way to forgive is to pour out my heart to God and ask Him to do it through me. As I pray this prayer, with tears rolling down my cheeks, telling God how much I hurt, I find He hears and answers. It's still somewhat of a process, but the process is accelerated, and I can altogether release it. Although I still remember what happened, it no longer matters. There is no sting; there is no pain when I think about it. In fact, I thank God that it happened because I can see the miracle he has performed in me.

Richard Foster reminds us in his classic *Celebration of Discipline* that the moment we feel we can succeed by the strength of our will alone, is the moment we begin worshipping the will. Willpower is simply not enough to enable us to succeed at forgiving someone who has hurt us deeply. It may, says Foster, produce an outward show of success for a while, but eventually our deep inner condition will be exposed. At some unguarded moment a slip of our tongue will reveal the true condition of our heart. "The will has the same deficiency as the law-it can only deal with externals. It is incapable of bringing about the necessary transformation of the inner spirit."[5]

After Pat chose to forgive, God showed her how to take the evil done to her family and work it for good. First, she and her family established a scholarship fund in Mark's memory for students in the Fort Myers area planning to go into music education as a career.

Then, Pat began to work with young men in detention (ages 18 to 22), ministering to the demographic that hurt her and her family so deeply. She also counsels fellow clergy members who have children that are incarcerated. How many scholarship recipients, young men in detention, and fellow clergy members whom Pat counsels are praising God for these ministries? Surely Pat's prayer the night her brother was murdered has been answered, "God, use this for your glory."

One of the greatest things about God is His ability to take

the evil and work it for good. If we just hand it to Him, He will show us, step by step, how to do that. Pat's ministry was deepened and expanded because of her experience. She herself has been through the dark valley of pain and suffering, learning that God can do through her what she is incapable of doing herself. She will use all she has endured to be a better counselor, comforter and minister. It's the only choice that makes sense.

Chapter Ten

Contemplating Suicide

Music, a Mentor and a Message from God

Collin McPherson, an introverted teenager, didn't fit in. He had a lot going for him – his parents loved him, took him to church, and sent him to private Christian school – but he felt he had no friends. He took seriously all his parents told him: set a good example, don't drink, respect authority; but sometimes he seemed to be the only person in his class that adhered to his parents' code of ethics. Other kids would either engage in conduct he could not condone (drinking, swearing, cheating) or would associate with him only during structured activities such as baseball practice.[1]

Collin was a good pitcher for the baseball team, but the coaches were negative, and he came to hate practices.

Instead of appreciating his hard work at practices and during games, the coaches criticized him. His quiet and awkward personality did not endear him to the other players, either, so Collin found no fulfillment in sports.

He did enjoy his church youth group. He loved the praise music and felt he belonged when he was with the other teens there. As soon as the youth meetings ended, however, he again felt alone, knowing it would be a week before the next youth meeting and the opportunity to associate with his peers in a nonthreatening environment.

At school, Collin developed a self-righteous attitude, seeing himself as a martyr, paying the price for clean behavior. Though he knew others judged him for being a "goody goody" he judged right back. The wall between Collin and his classmates grew higher by the day.

One day after baseball practice, Collin came home to an empty house. He sat down in the middle of the kitchen floor, the guest of honor at his own pity party. It had been a rough day at school and baseball practice had been brutal. He saw a knife on the kitchen counter and picked it up. Dark thoughts ran through his mind, *I can pay my coaches and my classmates back for their meanness and rejection. If I stab myself they'll be really sorry for their hateful attitudes at my funeral. They'll come and wish I were alive again and wish they hadn't been so critical.*

Although Collin didn't realize it at the time, the dark forces surrounding him were being countered. Collin's mother is a prayer warrior, and even though she was not at home, her prayers protected him at the lowest point in his life. Frank Perretti, in his novel, This Present Darkness[2], takes us behind the curtain of what we can't see with our physical eyes and what surely must happen when we're surrounded by prayer. The demons are held at bay and disbursed through the prayers of the saints. They complain that as long as the saints are praying, their work is greatly hindered.

C. S. Lewis agrees in *The Screwtape Letters*[3]. As Uncle Screwtape, the senior devil, is instructing his nephew, Wormwood, a novice devil, on how to operate in the world, he counsels what must be done if Wormwood should lose the major battle and his appointed subject should become a Christian. "At that point, whatever you do," says Screwtape, "keep him off his knees."

As Collin sat on the floor looking at the knife and contemplating suicide, something inside of him said, *Don't do it.* He thought about how much his parents and his brother loved him and how hurt they would be if he took his life. He found himself thinking, *There has to be something more. There has to be something out there for me.* Putting the knife back on the counter, he went upstairs to his room, still depressed.

At youth group that week his youth pastor, Andy, sensed something wasn't quite right and invited Collin to "lunch" after school. On the appointed day, Andy phoned to say he was in heavy traffic and running late, but Collin sat there for over an hour waiting on him because he was so desperate to talk to someone. When Andy finally arrived, Collin poured out his heart. In his own words, "Finally, there we were sitting together at a tall table towards the middle left side of the restaurant. I told him everything about everything going on in my life. I told him about my best pitching season ever for baseball, but how I still felt disconnected to most of the players and coaches on the team. I told him how my school life had grown to be structured solely around isolation and how my grades were the lowest they had ever been. I told him how some of my friends really cared more about alcohol and weed than chilling with me, and how I was at such a low point in my social life. I talked and talked. I couldn't stop talking. I never poured myself out like that to anyone, but the crazy thing about it was that the entire time I rambled on about my life, Andy listened. He looked me directly in the eyes, and he completely heard me out. And every time I reached a pause or breaking point, he would turn around with an overwhelming embrace of support and encouragement. He wasn't about to let me lose the battle, drop out of the race, or give anything less than my best. He cared about me, and it was through this love that my life was changed."

As Andy listened, asking questions to clarify and show Collin he understood, he finally had a chance to respond to Collin's diatribe. He reminded Collin he was not alone, though it felt like it. He reminded Collin of his future and told him this present situation would change.

After several hours with Andy, Collin felt as if the weight

of the world had been taken off of his shoulders. He sensed a purpose for his life and even found himself thinking that maybe he would be a youth pastor himself. For the first time in weeks, he felt accepted and loved by someone outside of his family, though he didn't give God credit until later.

Collin finished his school year and enjoyed the summer away from the pressure. He continued going to youth group and heard one of the adult leaders teach on mixing up your prayer life and experimenting with new ways to pray. She called it "spanking the dirt," based on how farmers in third world countries would spank the dirt to get it to produce. The lesson seemed to speak to Collin directly, so he started prayer walking at night after he finished his homework, listening to praise music and trying to see if he might hear God speak to him.

One night close to midnight after an especially rough week at school, he walked in desperation to his church. Collin said, "I decided to finish up my regular route with a stop in the courtyard next to the (church) sanctuary. I entered down its brick pathway and walked directly towards the tree centered perfectly in the square section of grass. As I leaned up against its beautiful trunk, I gradually sank to its foundation, looked up at the white steeple topped with a cross, and began to weep. Streams of tears covered my face – it was time for me to just let go. I leaned my head back to rest on the tree's bark and closed my eyes. Everything was black. Nothingness. But then there was something. It started off as a few dim figures, but as they became clearer, they formed a combination of fiery orange and yellow letters and numbers spelling out: 'Philippians 4:19.' Abruptly I opened my eyes. Did that really just happen? I had no idea what this verse was or might stand for. I rose quickly, made my way back home, and went straight to the family computer."

As Collin googled Philippians 4:19, he shook as he waited for the screen to open, and he found himself blown away when the words appeared, "And my God will meet all your needs according to his glorious riches in Christ Jesus."

Collin realized that it was God's message to him – right then, right there. He knew God understood where he was, was on his side, and would, in fact, do exactly what He had just said – provide for all of Collin's needs. The depression and fear vanished. Collin relaxed. That's what the cross was all about, he thought.

Collin kept listening to the praise music and kept trying to talk to God during his evening walks. On one of the church's local mission trips with the youth group, he struck up a conversation with Macy, a girl that went to his school and was a year ahead of him. He felt a connection with her, and Macy, being a committed Christian, invited him to join her in reading the Bible at school. She got Collin to take his faith seriously, and as they read and discussed God's word daily together, Collin began to feel an emotional attachment to her and invited her to the homecoming dance.

They had a wonderful time at the dance, but afterward Macy sat him down and told him he was putting his faith in her, not God. She told him he needed Christian brothers to encourage him and hold him accountable. As Macy slowly backed out of Collin's life, he again cried out to God – this time praying for the Christian brothers Macy said he needed, remembering God's promise, "My God will meet all your needs …."

Not too long thereafter, Collin went on the youth choir spring tour, rooming with two brothers and another guy who loved music and played the guitar. One night while on tour, they stayed up talking for hours, sharing their thoughts and dreams, hopes and fears. The evening ended in prayer, and the young men, amazed by how they felt God's presence with them, decided to get together back at church for weekly prayer meetings, inviting others to join them. They wrote a brochure called "Righting the Wrongs – A Youth Community Prayer Team" to get the word out. The brochure outlined the plan:

"From the outside looking in, what does this group signify and what do we plan on getting out of it? Let's first break down the name 'Righting the Wrongs.'

"At the beginning of life we are each born with the burden of original sin, a weight we must carry until we allow Jesus to intercede on our behalf. Unfortunately before that point is reached, our lives are sin filled, they are "wrong." This is not meant to discourage us, but it's meant for us to realize that there is something more to be found in life and that it is completely attainable. A hope that overcomes all earthly struggles.

"Finding Jesus in a person's life is a choice that an

individual must make on his or her own. It's a decision –
jumping in, staying in - all in. There is no sitting on the fence,
no 'maybes' or 'buts.' The truth is blatantly straightforward;
there is a 'right' way to live life which is through God and
there is a 'wrong' way to live life which is through everything
and anything else. Hence, we get our name, "Righting the
Wrongs."

"Now looking towards the future, we must discover what
every student needs when they take their first steps into the
real world. They each need strength to handle the many
difficulties thrown at them, motivation to continue in the
path God wants them to follow, and a prosperity of life in the
spirit.

"In summation, this group is designed to and will change
lives, it is designed to and will bring this youth community
closer together, and is designed to and will bring glory to
God in his mighty kingdom. This group has one rule which
is to follow the instructions that God leaves for us, no matter
the depths it takes us or the extremities he so chooses to
challenge us with. Now it's time for us to go out and make
disciples throughout the nations, leading the world to the
return of its savior and all of eternity."

During his senior year in high school, Collin led the
student group. No adults were allowed, not even twenty-
something year olds. His life found its purpose, and he knew
he was making a difference in the lives of others who felt
alone as he had felt.

Collin used a mentor and the power of healing music

and prayer walking to get him through many tough days and even years until he found his place and purpose as a teenager. In fact, God used the music to supply his need for emotional healing during the turbulent period of his life. Even King Saul, suffering from depression himself, called for David to strum the strings of the harp to counter the evil spirits. [4]

Barbara Crowe, past president of the National Association of Music Therapy, suggests the sounds and rhythm of music calm the constant chatter of the left brain, masking input from other senses, like vision, smell and touch. With the other senses subdued, the "normally noisy left brain" with its internal conversations, analyses and judgments, subsides, giving place to the deeper parts of the brain that are the "throne rooms" of symbols, visualizations and emotions.[5] [6]

Through praise and worship music, Collin dealt with his emotions and felt connected to God. By pouring his heart out to his youth pastor, a mentor, he rid himself of negative thoughts and hurt feelings and received encouragement and a more mature perspective on his life. With this transparency, he shifted part of his burden to other, stronger shoulders, realizing the blessing of letting another bear his burdens with him.

Now, on the other side of the years of despair and today a college sophomore, Collin writes: "God has met all my needs – every last one of them – and he continues to meet them each day. He took away the knife; he put Andy ... in my life; he sent me messages I needed to hear; [O]n the other side, I am now alive again as a child of God, standing in the world with a meaning and a purpose."

God has indeed restored the years of Collin's life that the locust destroyed.[7]

Chapter Eleven

Parenting Down Syndrome Children

Visualizing God's Presence
Blogging and Journaling

For parents with normal children, having a special needs child seems overwhelming. When Emily and John Kincaid had their second Downs Syndrome child, they wondered if God had lost all sense of fairness.[1]

Emily and John had been high school sweethearts. They married right out of college, and Emily supported them working as an office manager for an architect while John attended medical school. At the time, she believed her goal of continuing her education and getting a graduate degree in psychology was just being deferred. When they were finally in a position to start a family, they, as all young couples expecting for the first time, eagerly anticipated the arrival of their baby.

When baby Josh arrived, all Emily's plans changed. Josh was born with Down syndrome and several other physical problems. Before he was three, he had been hospitalized thirteen times with a number of surgeries, including surgery for a soft cleft palate. Emily found herself emotionally and physically exhausted as Josh did not sleep more than two hours at a time. For six years, Emily dealt with doctors, therapists and lack of sleep, until she felt things had stabilized to some extent.

Emily and John knew the odds of having a Down syndrome baby were remote, but just to make sure, they underwent genetic testing. They were told the chances of having a second Down syndrome child were about one in a million. Encouraged by these results, when Josh was six, they decided to try again, and Emily became pregnant. This time a beautiful daughter, baby Kimberly, was born into their family. At first, she seemed like any other newborn, but after a few days, Emily says she began to see characteristics in baby Kim she had seen in Josh. She asked herself, "Haven't we been through this before?"

Her pediatrician suggested tests, and the results hit hard. Baby Kim was a Down syndrome baby as well.

By this time, Emily and John had loved and cared for Josh for seven years, and knew he was incredibly special and precious. Yet, the thought of caring for two special needs children overwhelmed them. John was busy with his medical practice, and Emily had the primary responsibility for the children.

Emily's mother and sister provided help and support with the children when she needed to get out and get away. Her sister, riddled with health issues herself, lived with their mother and seemed to have a special gift when it came to caring for and relating to the children.

A neighborhood prayer group also provided spiritual strength and support for Emily as she gathered weekly with her neighbors to lift them up and allow herself to be lifted up in prayer to a gracious heavenly Father. Emily found God did, indeed, provide abundant courage, strength, wisdom and love to raise her special children.

While the neighborhood prayer group provided nurture and a Christian, social network, Emily reached up for her greatest needs. Every morning after John left for work and Emily got the children dressed and off for school, she had moments to herself. "I sat on the floor in the middle of the family room in my home," she says. "I closed my eyes and asked God to be with me, visualizing Him sitting there. I just wanted to be with Him and to affirm He was in control of my situation and my children. I put my children in His hands and asked Him to take care of them. I found I could leave them there with God at least for an hour or two each day, and this brought confidence and peace. Sometimes I would imagine myself sitting at His feet and other times we would sit on a hill and look down on earth, observing the scenes. I didn't want to ask Him for anything as much as I wanted to be with Him. I recognized He anguished with me and with all of us when we go through tough times. He showed me that He is the light of the world, and when we sit or stand with Him, we become conduits of His light."

"Because he loves me, says the Lord, I will rescue him. I will protect him for he acknowledges my name. He will call on me, and I will answer him; I will be with him in trouble. I will deliver him and honor him. With long life I will satisfy him, and show him my salvation."[2]

Kimberly presented different challenges for Emily, although, she too, had great difficulty sleeping. Her gastrointestinal tract didn't function well, and both of these problems intensified Emily's caregiving duties as she dealt with these problems along with everything else. "I put a mattress down in the middle of the floor of her room," says Emily. "I slept with her so she would get some sleep at night."

As Josh started public school, the challenges increased. In 1975, Congress had passed the Individuals with Disabilities Education Act, providing for children with disabilities to be included and made a part of the regular classroom educational experience for most of the day. Josh, as a result, was placed in a regular public school classroom and became the trial balloon for the program in his county, especially when he reached high school.

As many Down syndrome children did not continue to high school and because mainstreaming these children was still new, Josh's presence in the county high school as the first multi-handicapped person there, disturbed and angered some of his classmates. While teens tend to be self focused, the treatment Josh received was openly hostile. Between classes Josh was tortured, beaten on the head and threatened with a knife. His teachers would stand with him in the hall between classes so he would be safe. The school administration doubted Josh could complete high school, but Emily persisted. At one point she met with one of Josh's teachers for four and one half hours to persuade her Josh could and would endure and continue.

Every morning, Emily turned Josh over to God and prayed for his protection. She taught Josh that God and Jesus lived with him and would make a difference in his life and even his day. She showed him how to talk to God throughout the day and helped him to see the tangible benefit of prayer.

Emily's neighborhood prayer group continued to pray as well, and found prayer requests turning into praise reports. The teacher who doubted Josh's ability to even survive at the high school became Josh's biggest champion, realizing what Down syndrome children could do with adequate encouragement. And Josh was learning to pray himself through the challenges he faced throughout the day.

Even kings face open hostility. King David faced formidable enemies, spending days on end hiding in caves to escape them. "Give us aid against the enemy, for human help is worthless. With God we will gain the victory, and he will trample down our enemies."[3]

Emily says Josh learned to be non-judgmental of himself and to accept himself and others as God made them. It was as if Josh's high school classmates were learning the same lesson. Threats lessened, and Josh became a bona fide member of the class. When graduation approached, Emily was asked to provide a caption for Josh's senior picture in the yearbook. After considerable prayer, she wrote, "You fought the dragon and won." She said Josh loved it.

While Emily found her greatest help from private times of meditation and prayer throughout the day, Kelle Hampton, another mom of a Down syndrome child, found healing through writing and blogging.[4]

Kelle, a born extrovert, was the mother of a vibrant toddler when she called her husband and close friends to meet her at the hospital for the birth of her second child. Between contractions, Kelle and her support group chatted happily and eagerly anticipated the arrival of Kelle's baby. Finally, the contractions intensified, the friends left to wait outside, and Baby Nella Cordelia made her first appearance. The nurse handed her to

Kelle and said, "Here is your beautiful daughter."

Kelle immediately suspected something, but the nurses gave her no indication of any problems. Kelle's friends came back in and toasted Nella Cordelia, and her father offered a prayer of thanksgiving to God for his newest granddaughter. Kelle, despite joining in the festivities, worried little Nella did not seem quite right.

When Kelle's pediatrician finally arrived and examined her little patient, she asked everyone but Kelle and her husband to leave the room. Kelle says the doctor first knelt down so she could look up at Kelle and said, "The first thing I want to tell you is that your daughter is beautiful." She then told Kelle and her husband her suspicions that Nella was a Down syndrome baby and suggested testing to confirm.

When Kelle finally reached the point of writing about her experience, she shared her pain and how she screamed through the first night following Nella's birth. But her husband and everyone else in her life loved the new baby. Her friends assured her Nella was precious and would be treated as any other child of hers or theirs. When Kelle's sister arrived, she published a blog for Kelle and made her aware of her special place in the universe telling her she had a mission. Through family and friends, tears of pain turned to tears of joy, and Kelle began to see the beauty and opportunities her special baby presented.

Kelle's concerns for her older daughter, Lainey,

turned out to be groundless. Lainy embraced her little sister as if she were the most brilliant, talented baby ever born. She proudly wore her Big Sister hat her mother made for her and loved holding and kissing baby Nella.

Kelle's husband also lovingly embraced his new daughter, giving Kelle confidence as little Nella was accepted by every member of the family. Following Kelle's lead, he and big sister Lainey learned to look for the positives in every situation.

Kelle says, "I find much healing and growth in the process of writing to celebrate the good and recognize the beauty in our lives. I feel lucky; I feel privileged. I feel there is a story so beautiful in store. We will embrace this beauty and make something out of it."

Kelle's writes, she says, to help people see special needs in a different way, although she originally wrote for herself, finding healing through the writing down of her emotions. Through her writing, blogging and social networking, Kelle has helped other families going through similar (and even more difficult) experiences know everything will be all right. Emotional healing came to Kelle from sharing , reaching out and getting help from others.

On her path, Kelle stops to help those who have just begun the journey. But she also looks to those who are ahead of her on the same path and gleans from their wisdom and experience. She sows and reaps and teaches others to do the same.

Kelle epitomizes what the Apostle Paul wrote from his prison cell to the church at Phillipi. Bone tired from his many missionary journeys, threatened by the Roman authorities, questioned by his friends, Paul maintained a spirit of joy. He saw his imprisonment as an opportunity to witness to the prison guards and continue his ministry from where God had placed him. It seemed the more difficult life was for Paul, the happier he was. Less of stuff, more of God. From his jail cell, he wrote, " Whatever is true, whatever is noble, whatever is right, whatever is pure, whatever is lovely, whatever is admirable - if anything is praiseworthy - think on these things."[5]

With Kelle actively seeking the good and beauty in Nella and everything connected to her, it's no wonder God has brought Kelle and her husband to the place where they thank Him for the special privilege of raising a Down syndrome child. The love these children so unreservedly express touches the hearts of all they encounter. While we, with our egotistical natures, tend to think they will always need us as their teachers, in reality, they teach us far more than we can ever hope to teach them: loving without judgment and acceptance of themselves as they are.

Chapter Twelve

Dealing with Loneliness and Disabilities

Drawing Strength from our Furry Friends

*P*hyllis's life was falling apart. Her mother died after a long battle with cancer. Her boss, strapped by the recession, had to lay people off. She lost her job. Then, her marriage fell apart. She and her husband sold their home and separated. The only constant was her thirteen year-old Welsh Terrier, Trooper, which Phyllis had gotten as a pup. She and Trooper were devoted to each other, and, at a time when everything else in her life was unraveling, Trooper was there, God's instrument to remind her of His unconditional love .

Phyllis found herself back in the job market, looking for a place to live. Each time she would come home from an interview, exhausted, Trooper would be there to greet her. Phyllis hugged him, and buried her face in his fur. He stayed close, snuggling up to her if she sat down, and resting his head on her lap.

When Trooper stopped eating and became listless, his powerful body seeming to shrink, Phyllis became concerned and immediately contacted her vet, Dr. Guilliford. Dr. Guilliford met her as she pulled into his office, and lifted Trooper from the passenger seat in her car, carrying him into the examining room. As Phyllis followed along, she prayed fervently, asking God to let Trooper stay with her a little longer, reminding him that Trooper was all she had. She needed him, she told God, at least until she got her life back on track.

Dr. Guilliford ran tests, and, as he analyzed them, told Phyllis that Trooper was very, very ill with a liver malfunction. He started Trooper on intravenous fluids and medications, even arranging to spend the night at the clinic with him. "Go home," he told Phyllis. He told her he would call her in the morning and, by then, he should know if Trooper was going to make it.

Phyllis couldn't sleep. She prayed and cried all night, but when her phone rang at dawn, Dr. Guilliford told her what she wanted to hear. Although, he said, Trooper would need a special diet and extraordinary care, he would pull through. As Phyllis began to thank him, he stopped her, saying he had never seen a dog pull through this illness before. He told her something else was at work - that he was not responsible for Trooper's remarkable recovery, and he could not take the credit.

Phyllis then told her vet that she had been praying all night for Trooper.

Dr. Guilliford explained that Trooper's liver could not tolerate certain substances so she had to be careful about his food, but he looked so much better after a stay with Dr. Guilliford. Phyllis offered a prayer of thanks and promised God she would take good care of him.

Over the next two years, Phyllis rebuilt her life, landing a job on a newspaper and finding a house on an old estate where she and Trooper had plenty of room for long walks. She made new friends who cared about her, and through it all, Trooper's love strengthened her and gave her courage to go on.

Just about the time Phyllis had gotten back on her feet, Trooper's health began to fail. He lost his hearing. Then, he lost his sight, and felt threatened by everything except for Phyllis. Phyllis knew his time was up. With tears in her eyes she called Dr. Guilliford, "It's time," she said. Dr. Guilliford said he would wait for her at the clinic.

Phyllis put her arms around Trooper one more time, and, before she let him go, she lifted one more prayer, thanking God for her best friend who helped her through the most traumatic years of her life.[1]

I daresay that animals have helped the human race get through more crises than all the psychiatrists in the world combined. Dogs and cats, horses and birds, gerbils, dolphins, fish and rabbits bring comfort and companionship, often providing unconditional love for their human charges.

Volumes have been written about how animals have saved us, touched us, taught us, served us, comforted us, protected us, amused us, and met our needs in ways no human could possibly have done. In the best-selling memoir, *Marley and Me,* by John Grogan, Grogan credits Marley, their golden lab, with comforting his wife's heart when she miscarried their first child in a way no human could have. Marley stayed beside her, snuggled with her, kissed her and grieved with her in a way he was helpless to do.[2]

In this chapter I want to focus on three ways our pets and other animals help us through the tough times of our lives: Therapy and service dogs, horses used in rehabilitative programs, and what I'll call care-giving cats. I'm only scratching the surface, but no book on how people get through tough times would be complete without recognition and acknowledgment of our wonderful furry (and, in some cases, not so furry) friends.

THERAPY AND SERVICE DOGS

While therapy dogs and their human partners are involved in a wide range of activities such as visits to hospitals, visits to nursing homes, and listening to school-age children read, service dogs are specially trained to help people with disabilities. They assist those with visual and hearing impairments, mental illnesses, seizure victims, autistic persons, and diabetics. Service dogs are trained by service dog organizations.

For example, Service Dogs for America, located in Jud, North Dakota, trains dogs to "assist physically challenged individuals to gain greater independence and autonomy by use of a trained and certified assistance dog, and to do so without the financial burden to those using our program. The focus of our program is human service. The beneficiaries of our program are people."[3]

When five year-old, Conor, was diagnosed with congenital muscular dystrophy, his physical therapist suggested that a service dog might be helpful to him as he got older. His parents began to research various organizations and decided on Service Dogs for America. The family traveled to Jud, North Dakota and spent three weeks with several service dogs who were eager to go to work.

One of the dogs, Sheyenne, a young yellow lab, "chose" Conor, and "it was love at first sight" for both of them. Sheyenne has given Conor the independence he needs to walk without having to hold someone's hand and to be steady on his feet. If Conor falls and can't get back up, Sheyenne knows to push a button to alert his parents. When he drops something, she picks it up off the floor for him, and, perhaps most importantly, she stays with him as his constant companion when his friends run off to play.

For Conor's parents, Sheyenne provides a sense of security, knowing their son is never without assistance. Conor is able to lead an independent life because of this special canine friend, whom he has come to love and trust.[4]

Another organization that trains service dogs, Service Dogs for Independence, trained a golden retriever/poodle mix named Rex. Two veterans, just returning home from Afghanistan, needed help with their six year-old autistic son, Jamey. Jamey doesn't speak, but he loves to run, especially away from his mother. That's where Rex comes in, charging after Jamey and stopping him. Rex is even being trained to sniff out Jamey wherever he may be.

Jamey's mom had been trying to find a dog to assist Jamey, but knew they would need help financially. She and her husband tried to fundraise through Facebook, and then, one day got a call. "We're going to fund your dog." The call came from Veteran's United Foundation, a company whose employees donate one percent of their own salaries in order to help veterans and military families. They contributed eleven thousand dollars ($11,000) to help Jamey's family get Rex.

"There's no amount of money that compares to knowing Jamey is okay every minute of the day," says Christine, Jamey's mom. "Last night I slept really, really well."[5]

Holly is another service dog, assisting Lisa, who suffers from seizures. One day Lisa was at the grocery store in a manual wheelchair because her electric wheelchair was in the shop. Holly warned Lisa of an oncoming seizure, but because she was away from home, she did not have her medication. Her ride was late, and, as she waited, helpless to take the medication she needed, she had the seizure right outside the grocery store. As Lisa was in a catatonic state, her wheelchair began to roll towards the oncoming traffic in front of the store. Although she had not been trained to do it, Holly jumped up on Lisa, who was still in a coma from the seizure, and stopped the chair. Had Holly not gotten it to stop, says Lisa, she could have been killed, as the chair continued on its path headed right into the traffic.[6]

Dogs seem to know intuitively what their owners need and to be ready, willing and able to provide it, even to their own detriment. Don, a victim of ALS or Lou Gehrig's disease, which progressively causes loss of muscle function, was out one day with his wife Pat in a wheelchair. The family dog, Moby, was along and sat on Don's lap (as Moby did most of the time). As Pat was pushing Don along, a small animal caught Moby's attention. Moby bounded off of Don's lap and raced after it. There was nothing Pat could do to stop him. He could have become a permanent animal chaser at that point, had he so desired, but suddenly, he stopped dead in his tracks, looked back at Don and trotted back to the wheelchair, jumping right back up. It was as if Moby was saying, "You need me, Don, and I'm willing to give up any fun I might otherwise have in order to help you."[7]

HORSES

While many dogs are counted as members of their human families, horses, being too large to live in our homes, play a different role. I was first exposed to "equine therapy" on a trip out west with my sister. We enrolled in a class where we worked with horses to help us identify negative emotions, such as fear, that we might be projecting without knowing it. The trainer explained to us that the horses pick up on these emotions, and will signal to us if they sense them. The experience taught me how helpful our hoofed friends can be to help us overcome damaging vibrations we inadvertently emit.

Equine therapy is also used to help handicapped and disabled persons regain a sense of freedom and mobility. At the Pegasus Riding Academy in Philadelphia, PA horses provide hope, therapy and fun to stroke victims, handicapped persons, and those with mental disabilities. The center receives referrals from more than forty area health agencies, rehabilitation centers, hospitals and schools for children with disabilities.

The Pegasus web site explains that the movement of the horse has proven to be very effective in helping people establish balance, coordination and perception when compared to static treatments. The horse's movement is three dimensional, rhythmic, and repeatable, all movements needed to simulate normal walking patterns. The horse's gait closely resembles the human gait and helps physically challenged children discover the rhythm they need to begin taking steps on their own. The horse's movement stimulates the brain and neurological system as well as the hips and legs, preventing atrophy of walking muscles if walking is not possible.

Horses are also helpful with children who have been diagnosed as autistic. Horses and children with autism interpret the world pictorally, making the horses more in sync with these special children. As the bond becomes stronger, eye contact, facial recognition, and interaction become possible with many riders.[8]

At another riding academy for the disabled, one instructor notes that men in particular find a horse bolsters their spirits. "Here they are all John Wayne," she says. "If they can do exercise and therapy on a horse, it's more fun and something they consider manly and out of doors."[9] When they talk to their friends who play golf or tennis they can say they went horseback riding.

CATS

My husband and I have two dogs, but we used to have cats when our daughter was young. My brother gave us a cat he was not allowed to keep in his college dormitory room, and Tigger, a young black and gray striped feline, became part of our family. That cat was the sibling our daughter never had, sleeping with her at night, sitting on her bed while she did her homework, and greeting her when she got home from school. She loved Tigger so much we eventually had three cats, to my husband's amazement, because he thought he was allergic to cats.

One of our cats loved to chase the neighbor's cat up trees which upset our neighbor terribly. We tried everything, but that cat just kept finding a way to get out and run after his feline neighbor. I finally realized we would have to find a new home for Socks, the cat. I put an ad in the paper and got a call from a little boy who wanted to know what color the cat was and whether it was an inside or an outside cat. I could tell he, like our daughter, wanted an animal to love. I asked him to put his mother on the phone. She told me her son did, in fact, want a pet to keep him company in the afternoons when he came home from school. She was a working mom, and he was an only child.

"Coincidentally" the mother worked in the same building where I worked, so we agreed that I would bring Socks on loan for a weekend to see how he did. I worried about Socks all weekend, hoping he and Billy, her son, were getting along. Monday morning Billy's mother showed up at my office at 9:00. "Billy's beside himself with joy over that cat. He's been getting up 15 minutes early every morning to scramble Socks an egg. He adores Socks, and Socks seems happy. We're going to keep him." Once again our cat was providing love and companionship to a child. I told my husband, "Socks moved from the Days Inn to the Ritz Carlton. I never got up every morning to cook him an egg."

Although cats are generally regarded as more aloof than dogs, they can be great caregivers in their own right. My friend, Terry, was hit by a careless driver while he was crossing a downtown street, in the crosswalk, with the light in his favor. Terry catapulted through the air landing on concrete. He sustained serious injuries requiring a permanent neck brace and great loss of mobility, forcing him to give up his lucrative law practice. When I visited him at his home some time after the accident, I met Oscar, a huge orange cat that must have weighed 25 pounds. Oscar spread himself out on the sofa next to Terry's chair and gave me the initial impression of being pretty useless. I was quite surprised when Terry and his lovely wife, Karen, told me Oscar's story.

Terry had not wanted a cat, but when their daughter, then in college, was about to become a teenager, Karen told Terry they needed to get a cat for her to love. The wheels in Terry's mind started turning, "It's the cat or the boys," he thought.

"How many cats do you want?" he asked Karen. They adopted Oscar. Although they got Oscar for their daughter, after Terry's accident, Oscar became Terry's cat. Oscar can be rambling around the house minding his own business, running into the yard, chasing squirrels or doing whatever else cats do amuse themselves, but as soon as the rest of the family leaves, he takes up his post and stays right with Terry until the family returns. Oscar knows Terry needs him, and he intends to be there.

Oscar and Terry have a special bond, and at a time when Terry should be interacting with colleagues at the office, Oscar provides a special kind of companionship: loyal, loving, and steadfast.[10]

Animals are a gift from God – in good times and bad – and in our darkest hours, it is often our pets who are and remain our best friends. With no agenda other than to minister to us when we most need their love, they are there, knowing they're needed and willingly giving their all.

General Trauma

Chapter Thirteen

Confronting Challenge and Controversy - Paying the Price To Stand By Firming Held Convictions

Sustained by Deep, Moral Convictions

*E*ven peripheral students of American history know about the bloody Civil War we fought over the issue of slavery from 1861 to 1865. Slavery was abolished and the war ended, but the conflict continued. For a century thereafter, African-Americans were treated with scorn and contempt, relegated to some kind of second class citizenship status. Southern restaurants served them only at back doors, refusing to allow blacks to sit at tables in the main establishment. Blacks had to go to the rear of buses and sit behind the whites. Blacks and whites were segregated – in schools, on playgrounds and at other public facilities. Even the United States Supreme Court, in its 1896 decision of *Plessy v. Ferguson*[1] held (in a 7-1 majority opinion) that state laws requiring "separate but equal" facilities for blacks and whites were constitutional. *Plessy v. Ferguson* remained good law until 1954 when a unanimous Supreme Court, headed by Chief Justice Earl Warren, overturned it in *Brown v. Topeka Board of Education*[2] declaring "separate but equal educational facilities inherently unequal." Racial segregation was thereby ruled a violation of the equal protection clause of the 14th Amendment of the U.S. Constitution.

Although the law had changed, the hearts and minds of many U.S. citizens had not. States in the deep South threatened to close schools rather than integrate. In September, 1957 when nine African-American students enrolled in Little Rock, Arkansas' Central High School, Arkansas Governor Orval Faubus ordered the Arkansas National Guard to surround the school to keep them out. Then President Dwight D. Eisenhower sent the 101st Airborne Division into Little Rock to ensure the safety of the "Little Rock Nine" and to uphold the ruling of the U.S. Supreme Court.[3]

As states came to grips with the new law of integration, several engaged in foot-dragging policies, spending millions of dollars in legal fees to defer integration of schools as long as possible. Tests were administered, requiring African-

American students to obtain certain scores before allowing them to attend white schools. Grades were integrated one per year. In some states, all the dilatory tactics that could be devised were used.

Schools were not the only battleground. When Rosa Parks of Montgomery, Alabama refused to give up her bus seat to a white passenger in 1955, she was arrested, and the incident catapulted the Civil Rights Movement to a new level of intensity. A young Baptist minister, the Reverend Dr. Martin Luther King, Jr., became its spokesman, leading a bus boycott in Montgomery that lasted over three hundred days.

As the eloquent Dr. King continued to advocate for equal treatment for blacks, traveling extensively to get his message across to a nation whose collective heart was still hardened, he moved his ministry to Atlanta, Georgia where he could more easily get to any other city to which he was called.

Despite continuing threats to his life and that of his family and a fire-bombing of his personal residence, he lived up to his namesake, Dr. Martin Luther, the German scholar, in every respect. Martin Luther, founder of the protestant church, protested abuses in the Catholic church which included sales of indulgences to enrich church coffers. He posted his famous Ninety Five Theses, setting forth these abuses, in 1517. When asked to recant, Luther replied "Here I stand. I can do no other."[4]

Dr. King became an international hero, winning the Nobel Peace Prize in 1963. His advocacy of nonviolent opposition to racial inequality in the face of great danger to his life and that of his family earned him the same respect and admiration accorded to William Wilberforce, the British politician who led the movement to abolish slavery in Great Britain, and Mahatma Gandhi, who became the leader of Indian nationalism, advocating a non violent approach to independence in India.

Although Dr. King was the leader of the Civil Rights movement, he was by no means the only one who paid a high price for the injustices that confronted him daily. A few brave white southerners sacrificed reputations, friendships, business and social successes to join him in the fight.

In the 1950s, when the Civil Rights movement was heating up, Sara Perry Mitchell was an Atlanta socialite, who played bridge and went to garden and study clubs while she raised her three children. Weekends were spent at her successful husband's country club. While she seemed happy enough, something deep inside her was starting to stir, asking her if she wanted her children to remember her by what a good bridge player she was.[5]

Sara came to regard the Civil Rights Movements as the "Second Battle of Atlanta," and while she had been spared the first one, she enlisted herself and became a fierce fighter, alongside Dr King, in the second one.[6]

Sara had been raised in a middle-class Southern home where a black cook raised white children and did the laundry for unconscionably low wages. Whites had every reason to want to preserve the status quo. As a young wife and mother she herself employed a black nurse/housekeeper who accompanied the family on vacations. Once, in the 1940s, when going through Alabama to New Orleans, the family stopped at a local restaurant for lunch. Letha, the black nurse, went in holding one of Sara's babies. Sara thought there would be no problem since Letha was wearing a uniform, but she was wrong. The owner walked over and said, "We don't serve her kind. She's got to leave."[7]

Sara asked herself, *Why should she suffer such an indignity just because of the color of her skin?* The sense of injustice that hit her at that moment began to take root and would later blossom into a firm conviction that such discrimination, prejudice and hatred could not be allowed to continue. Indeed, it was this strong conviction that carried her through the disapproval of her husband, friends, and family as she seized the torch of justice and equality for all and marched through her City, as passionate as any Old Testament prophet, calling the people to repent and turn.

Sara's oldest son shocked her when he reported that his friend's father, a close neighbor, had a Ku Klux Klan robe and hood in his closet. She could take it no longer, and determined then and there to move into action. She sat down and wrote letters of resignation to her two bridge clubs, her garden club and her study club. There had to be something more significant for her to do. Her friends protested, telling her that she was ruining her only daughter's chance to make her debut,[8] but Sara moved forward regardless and with intentionality.

About that same time, Sara was asked to chair a new committee at her church: The Status of Women Committee. She agreed, and immediately set out to get the women registered to vote (only about 30 percent were registered at that time). Calling the League of Women Voters for help, she began helping the women to have a voice. Sara writes, "From this point in 1953 onward, the steps in my long journey from complacent, middle class Southern housewife to liberal, integrationist and politician came much more quickly. Once I started looking more closely at the world around me, I could never go back. In fact, what I saw made me realize that I could actually make a difference in the causes I believed in."[9]

Sara joined the League of Women Voters and quickly became chair of the education committee, leading the study of civil rights as applied to public education following the Brown v. Topeka Board of Education decision. League meetings were proceeding along as usual until a new member who had transferred from the North proposed a change in the by-laws, "I see this Chapter's bylaws don't conform to the National League's. Your bylaws state that any white woman may be a member....I move that the word "white" be stricken from the by-laws of the Atlanta League of Women Voters."[10]

Bedlam followed, but the motion narrowly passed. The Chapter's president, vice-president and six board members resigned. Sara was elected vice-president; four outstanding black women joined, and began sharing the many, many problems they were encountering in their segregated neighborhoods: crowded housing, unpaved streets, lack of city water. Any problems on the white side of town paled by comparison.

One of the black members joined the League's education committee to serve with Sara. Through her advocacy for black schools, Sara's "social life" became both controversial and public. Forgetting her former shyness, she began debating city council members, county commissioners, state legislators and even the governor of the State of Georgia, often finding her face on the front page of the Atlanta Journal.[11]

Back on the home front, these new activities created tension. Sara's husband was becoming increasingly intolerant of her vocal League involvement. She tried to appease him and rarely mentioned what she did while he went to work, but when her name kept appearing in the paper, the gulf between them widened.

In March, 1958 Sara was elected president of the Atlanta League for a two year term, leading the charge to persuade the Atlanta School Board to adopt a desegregation policy and pushing for funds to be more equitably distributed among white and black schools.[12] The League's work paid off, and after the City's first schools were successfully integrated, President John F. Kennedy called Georgia Governor Earnest Vandiver with congratulations.[13]

Although the initial "integration" of ten black students into five Atlanta high schools went smoothly, much remained to be done. The city's leading black newspaper published an editorial stating, "Nobody does us a favor when he grudgingly doles out to us a fraction of our rights. Atlanta must turn away from the congratulations and autograph parties and come to grips with the terrible inequalities that are crippling thousands of our innocent children.[14]

Sara knew the writer spoke truth, and she decided to run for the school board because of her convictions as a Christian, her expertise with the League of Women Voters, and her friendship with many blacks that led her to believe she could help.

She had one initial problem: She knew her husband would not approve, and she needed him to give her one thousand dollars to pay the ballot entrance fee. She did what any smart woman would have done – fixed him a delicious dinner and afterwards said, "Some wives whose husbands are in your income bracket ask for expensive jewelry or a mink coat. What I want is one thousand dollars to run for the Board of Education."[15] She got the money.

After enlisting the aid of a veteran campaign manager, Sara won her race. She was ready to roll up her sleeves and get to work, but any encouragement she received came from outside her home. She never shared her views on civil rights with her husband, nor did he with her, but she knew they were miles apart on the issue. Sara saw her once happy marriage eroding in front of her eyes.

Sara was also disgusted with the Southern churches, which, at a time they were "most needed for their Christianity," failed miserably in her eyes. She couldn't understand why they didn't step up to the plate and lend a collective loud cry against segregation. "So in Christ Jesus you are all children of God through faith, for all of you who were baptized into Christ have clothed yourselves with Christ. There is neither Jew nor Gentile, neither slave nor free, nor is there male nor female, for you are all one in Jesus Christ."[16] She recalled the words of Martin Luther King, Jr., "I have looked at the South's beautiful churches with their lofty spires pointing heavenly. Over and over I have found myself asking, 'What kind of people worship here? Who is their God?'"[17]

Sara, a member of a wealthy suburban protestant church, asked herself why it didn't feed and clothe the needy children of the city. She concluded, "The wealthy churches were building million dollar sanctuaries and large recreational centers with buses to carry privileged children to sporting events where they could compete with other over-privileged children."[18]

In a speech to a black college, Sara told the audience, "White churches have sinned so greatly in their treatment of blacks, they would not recognize the truth now if it came marching down the street." When these accusations and her picture landed on the front page of the Atlanta Journal, her husband made no attempt to hide his anger. Some letters to the editor, however, praised her courage.[19]

Meanwhile, as Sara began her first term on the School Board in January 1962, she encountered some unexpected opposition. The Board consisted of seven white men, one black man, Dr. Rufus Clement, president of Atlanta University, and Sara. Some of the white men represented the major banks in Atlanta that invested school funds. Sara, somewhat naïve about the way boards worked, jumped right in – pushing for more equal distribution of funds to black schools and taking upon herself the responsibility of personally visiting every school under the Board's jurisdiction, black and white. In doing so, she saw firsthand the lie of the separate but equal doctrine because black schools were nowhere nearly as well equipped or maintained as white schools. Sara made proposals expecting support of the lone black Board member – at least a second to her motions to improve black schools. When he did not ever support her, after several attempts, she went into him privately and asked why. "Mrs. Mitchell," he said, "Men do not like women who make decisions." Sara, stunned by his response, had to come to grips with the reality that black men could be just as chauvinistic as white men.[20]

Though Sara found herself alone in a sea of opposition, the black community recognized her as their sole friend on the Board. One young black civil rights activist told her, "Just seeing you sitting there makes us feel good."[21] She continued to push for elimination of double sessions in black schools, up-to-date textbooks, and basic necessities, such as a science lab in one of the black high schools. One author profiled her perfectly: "In many southern cities at least one courageous school official sought to counteract the object lesson in sophisticated dishonesty on display before the children. In Atlanta it was Sara Mitchell, who rose up in one of those moments of wrath that come upon moderate prophets. She fought with typical members of such a Board, mostly businessmen, mostly opposed in spirit, to the meaning of real education."[22]

Sara continued her advocacy and was reelected to a second term on the Board. She also changed churches, and began attending Ebenezer Baptist Church, home church of Martin Luther King, Jr. Sara wrote letters of encouragement to Dr. King, and on July 25, 1963 he wrote back: "I can assure you that your encouraging words give me new courage and vigor to carry on in this struggle to make the brotherhood of man a reality and bring the American dream to full realization. Let me also take this opportunity to express my deep appreciation for the courageous stand you are taking on the Atlanta School Board for the cause of brotherhood and integration. I appreciate your strong, forthright statements far more than words can express."[23]

The strong stands and publicity came with a high cost – Sara's marriage finally dissolved. She could not continue in a relationship that involved constant disapproval of her every word and action. She moved out of the home she loved into a small apartment, questioning whether or not she had done the right thing. As traumatic as the divorce proved to be, Sara years later wrote, "As I recall this time in my life today…I am once again aware that all of [my husband's] hostility centered on my open, active support of the Civil Rights Movement. How differently my life from age forty on would have been if I had not become a civil rights activist. Yet I know that I could never have lived differently. None of us can truly feel good about ourselves if we don't honor our deepest convictions."[24]

Sara Mitchell found those convictions strong enough to carry her through all the hurtful words and disapproval of so many in her sphere of influence. Sometimes conviction is all we have, conviction that truth and justice are more important than popular opinion, conviction that our discomfort is worth the price we are paying to stand up for what is right. It seems true prophets have always done that. Sara added her voice to that of Dr. King in her day and to that of the Old Testament prophet, Amos, in calling for justice to roll down like waters and righteousness as an ever-flowing stream.[25]

Chapter Fourteen

Financial Distress

Managing Money According to God's Word

G ary and Drenda Keesee were far too typical of young couples who find themselves buried in debt without visible means of getting out. They borrowed money to get married, and Gary went to work as a salesman paid on a commission only basis. Not knowing a lot about people, his sales were slow. Without a regular paycheck, the young couple resorted to using credit cards when they needed food, gas or other essentials. Even credit cards were insufficient to meet their needs, so they borrowed from relatives, borrowed against their cars, and took out finance company loans (at exorbitant interest rates).

Their home was falling apart. Broken windows, peeling

paint, and cracked window frames reminded them daily of their desperate situation, which caused great stress and anxiety, increasing with the arrival of babies.

With a negative net worth, Gary cried out to God, begging for help. Almost immediately, a verse of scripture popped into his mind, "And my God will meet all your needs according to thine riches of his glory in Christ Jesus." (Philippians 4:19)

God showed Gary that he had been relying on the world's financial system instead of God's plan for provision, and that it was time to stop sliding down the slippery slope of debt and start looking to God for the family's needs. Gary immediately told God he didn't have the money to get his car repaired, and that it would be better if it just burned up so he could collect the insurance. Within minutes of sharing this insight, Gary pulled into his driveway to see flames bursting from the hood of his car, engulfing the front of it. He immediately called the fire department, which rushed out and hosed down the charred heap. The car was totaled, and a check from the insurance company was delivered the next day to cover the loss. Gary used that check to pay off a creditor about to sue him, to pay the balance due on the car loan, and to pay off some smaller debts. He and Drenda were even able to buy some groceries with the rest of the funds. Not long thereafter a friend from church gave them a car that they no longer needed. God had made His point.

Gary and Drenda committed to stop using debt, to pay off their existing debt, and to start looking to God to provide whatever their family needed. One night, after prayer, Gary felt God was showing him to start his own business. To make a long story short, Gary and Drenda followed that lead, and slowly began to work their way out of the financial pit they had dug. God continued to give them wisdom in running the business, and they soon had to hire help. In looking to God for their needs and direction, in time they paid off all their debts and began to prosper. It wasn't quick; it wasn't pain-less; it didn't come without sacrifice; but it worked.[1]

In times of financial crises, the first step is looking to God, not debt, to meet our needs. If we are in debt, we need to commit to pay off our creditors. People or corporations lend us money trusting that we will pay it back. Paying it back is the only right and fair thing to do, no matter how long it takes or how hard it is. God does not want us in debt,[2] and he does want us to pay off our existing debt.[3] Financial guru, Dave Ramsay, has a great way of tackling debt. List every creditor we have starting with the smallest one, he advises. For example our list might look something like this:

Friend Joe at work: ....$ 100.00
Aunt Thelma: ....$ 1,000.00
Cousin Bill: ....$ 2,143.54
Ford Dealership: ....$ 3,167.13
Chevrolet Dealership: ....$ 4,679.38
Discover Card: ....$ 4,997.65
Visa Card: ....$ 5,133.18
Master Card: ....$ 5,567.85
Student Loan: ....$ 40,395.55

Home Mortgage: ....$ <u>150,867.25</u>

Total: ....$ 218,051.53

We first pay off Joe. Joe (probably never expecting to see that money again) is pleased, but, more importantly, we have a sense of accomplishment. We have paid off a debt and can strike it off the list. Then, we tackle Aunt Thelma's debt. This will take longer, but she, too, will be pleasantly surprised. We'll strike another debt off our list. Paying off the smaller debts first gives us confidence that with God's help, we can pay off the larger ones as well.[4]

From my own experience, I can tell you that when my husband and I paid off our own version of Aunt Thelma, the rewards were tremendous. Thirty-eight years later, when our "Aunt Thelma" passed away, we were the recipients of a bequest that far exceeded what we had borrowed from her and repaid. Through repayment, we gained credibility in Aunt Thelma's eyes.

Having learned to trust God for our needs, and get out of debt, we must also tap into a powerful spiritual law. I will share from my own experience about how my husband and I came to discover the truth of this biblical mandate.[5]

Years ago when I was called to law school we were faced with law school tuition at a private school and no income. My husband, home from a three-year tour of duty in the Navy, had just started a new firm with two of his law school buddies. At that point, they had no clients.

We realized we needed a radical financial plan. We also knew if the vision was from God (and believed it was) he would provide, but we didn't know how. We had heard of the concept of tithing, which as far as we knew meant giving ten percent of all of our income to the Lord's work. We decided a radical financial plan would be to give ten percent of anything we received to our church. That was it. Either tithing worked or it didn't. There was no Plan B. If tithing didn't work, I would not be able to go to school.

We stood on God's word in Malachi 3:10, "Bring the whole tithe into the storehouse, that there may be food in my house. Test me in this, says the Lord Almighty, and see if I will not throw open the floodgates of heaven and pour out so much blessing that there will not be room enough to store it."

This was quite a switch from our normal mode of giving, which was to put five dollars in the offering plate about once a month. We were desperate, however, and desperate times require desperate measures.

What happened the next three years (the law school years), was nothing short of financial miracle. I've often said it would have been worth those three years in law school even if I had never practiced law a day in my life just to see God working out the miracle for us. All the while my husband was in his brand-new law practice with his two buddies, taking whatever work they could get, with no security at all.

The first thing that happened to us was my mother-in-law's review of her financial records. She discovered she had spent more educating her daughter than her son (my husband) and wanted to even the score. So, she sent my husband a check to make everything perfectly equal. Wow! I was impressed. We gave ten percent to the church and used the rest for law school tuition.

Thereafter, various relatives would send checks to us in the mail, probably because they had heard of our absolutely crazy endeavor and felt sorry for us. Aunt Mary in New York would send checks from time to time – always a two or three-page letter which we couldn't read (because her handwriting was illegible). But we could read the check. My precious grandparents sent checks. Cousin Harriet, on the faculty at the University I attended, arranged for student loans for me through the loan office. And after I made it through the first year without them my wonderful sweet parents sent significant checks to help.

I remember vividly one Friday afternoon sitting in my car outside the law school. Tuition was due on Monday morning and we didn't have it "Lord," I prayed, "I'm putting this problem in your hands. If you want me to finish please send me the money. If you don't it's fine with me, but if you do I need (I named the amount of tuition)."

As soon as I had finished praying, I remembered we would be tithing on anything we received and the amount I had asked for wouldn't be enough. But God was ahead of me. On Saturday morning, I went to the mailbox and there was a check for an amount of money that after tithing, was exactly what we needed for tuition. Were we ever impressed!

In the meantime, back at the struggling new law practice, my husband had a client in the nursery business. Every time he and his wife came to Atlanta to see their lawyer, they brought boxes of fresh vegetables – tomatoes, cucumbers, squash and okra. The first time my husband brought their gifts home, I began spreading the vegetables out in the kitchen. I filled up our refrigerator and my kitchen table with them. All of my countertops were covered and I looked down at the boxes. There were still more vegetables. I didn't know where to put them. The words of Malachi rang loudly and clearly in my mind, "Bring all the tithes and ... see if I will not open the floodgates of heaven and pour out so much blessing there will not be room enough to store it." I sat down and cried, and then I began giving away vegetables to our neighbors.

By the time I had gotten to my third year of law school, I promised God that if he would keep miraculously providing the money for tuition for me to finish and the money for us to live on, I would seize any opportunity I could to tell people to tithe. In fact, I believe God led me into the area of estate and charitable planning so that I could do this professionally and help people plan to give some of their resources to the wonderful charitable organizations in this country (and worldwide).

My husband and I came to realize during those three years that tithing was the wisest investment we could make from every standpoint. We knew it would never, ever stop. And as a result, we have continued to see financial miracles in our lives. God is faithful to his word.

In tithing, we acknowledge that God owns it all. The

ten percent we give back to him is our recognition of his ownership. Think about how incredibly generous God is compared to any earthly employer or creditor. Have you ever heard of a creditor who only expected to get ten percent of the loan back (with no interest)? Or, have you ever heard of an employer who only required an employee to give back ten percent of the amount fronted by the employer? Yet, that is all God asks.

While God doesn't force us to tithe, he tells us if we don't tithe, we are robbing him, and if we rob him, we will be under a curse.[6] But, when we do "bring the whole tithe in the storehouse" he will "throw open the flood gates of heaven and pour out so much blessing that we will not have room to store it."[7] The passage goes on to say God will protect what we have from pestilence and other dangers if we bring the tithe in obedience.

As powerful as the spiritual law of tithing is, there is another law even more powerful – going beyond the tithe, or giving offerings. You see, we are commanded to tithe, and we suffer the consequences if we don't, but our offerings are a free will gift. We give because we want to, out of our love and devotion to God. Luke 6:38 says:

"Give and it will be given to you. A good measure, pressed down, shaken together and running over, will it be poured into your lap. For with the measure you use, it will be measured to you."

The Bank of God is the only bank offering decent interest rates these days.

The Prophet Elijah lived in the middle of a famine. God told him to go to a town called Zarephath where a widow would supply him with food. As Elijah approached the town gate, he saw a widow gathering sticks and asked her for water and a piece of bread. She replied, "As surely as the Lord your God lives, I don't have any bread - only a handful of flour in a jar and a little oil. I am gathering a few sticks to take home and make a meal for myself and my son, that we may eat it and die."[8]

The great prophet knew she needed to give up what she had in order for God to supply what she needed. He told her to first make a cake for him and bring it to him, and then her flour would not be used up and her jug of oil would not run dry for as long as the famine lasted. The widow did as Elijah instructed and tapped into the law of providential provision. She had flour and oil for herself and her son in keeping with the prophecy of Elijah.

In the recent business best seller, *Give and Take*, Adam Grant tells some powerful stories about givers who attributed their successes to their generosity. One of these entrepreneurs is Jon Huntsman, Sr., who started a chemical company that today reigns as the world's largest. He is one of just nineteen people in the world to have given away one billion dollars or more. When Huntsman's company tanked along with the industry in 2001, he lost a significant part of his fortune, but that did not deter his giving or his fulfillment of his charitable pledges. In order to make good on every one of them, he took out a personal loan.

Grant points out that while it looks like Huntsman got rich and then decided to give back, it could have been the other way around. What, asks Grant, if we've mixed up cause and effect?

Huntsman himself believes that being a giver actually made him rich. Remarkably, there is evidence to support this claim. The economist Arthur Brooks tested the relationship between income and charitable giving. Using data from almost thirty thousand Americans in the year 2000, he controlled for every factor imaginable that would affect income and giving. He adjusted for education, age, race, religious involvement, political beliefs and marital status. As expected, higher income led to higher giving. For every one dollar in extra income, charitable giving went up by fourteen cents. But, something much more interesting happened. For every one dollar in extra charitable giving, income was three dollars and seventy five cents higher. Giving actually seemed to make people richer....[9]

When we face financial crises, the good news is there are powerful spiritual laws, tithing and giving beyond the tithe, we can use to tap into supernatural provision. We must do our part, however, to honor God by staying obedient to His word. This might be tough for a while, especially if we have debt. As we move through the crises, in obedience, we can expect God to guide with insight, provision for our needs, and ideas. I do believe it is in our financial lives that we have the greatest opportunity to see God work in miraculous ways as we simply follow the guidelines He has provided.

Chapter Fifteen

Trapped Underground For 69 Days

Finding Power in Hope and Humor

f ever a note caused the world to rejoice, it was the cryptic message taped to a drill bit that found its way to an underground cavern harboring thirty three Chilean miners, trapped by a mine cave in seventeen days earlier on August 5, 2010. Chilean President Sebastian Pinera read the message, printed in bold red letters, to the media, "We are well in the shelter – the 33." Until the note returned, no one knew if the miners had survived the disaster at the 121-year-old San Jose copper-gold mine in northern Chile, near Copiapo. The thirty three men were trapped a half-mile underground, about three miles from the mine's entrance. As efforts to find the miners involved drilling down at different points, hoping for some response, when the note surfaced with the drill bit, it was like finding the mother load in a gold mine.

The news that all thirty three were alive and well brought tears of joy and relief to their families, friends and total strangers above ground, as well as dances of jubilation below because the miners knew what the news to those above meant. Rescue efforts would focus and intensify. Chances of surviving the crisis had just increased dramatically.

Families of the miners had set up tents near the mine's entrance (dubbed "Camp Hope") to watch, wait, and pray for the safe return of their husbands, fathers, sons and brothers. As a world watched on television, the families, many of whom were devout Catholics, prayed fervently. Volunteers came to help prepare meals, entertain children, and offer comfort and support. Once they knew the miners had survived the cave-in and waited to be rescued, they intensified pressure on the Chilean government to do everything possible to reach the men. Three large drilling rig teams, experts from the NASA Space Agency in the United States, and more than a dozen multi-national corporations assisted in the rescue operation.[1] Offers of help poured in from around the world.

As rescue efforts intensified above, still with no idea what method would be successful in reaching the miners and getting them back to the surface, the miners below faced many challenges. For the first seventeen days, they did not know if they would be found, much less rescued. Forty-year-old Mario Sepulveda, one of the older trapped miners, felt a responsibility to protect and encourage the younger ones. He called the initial seventeen day wait a "nightmare," as the men feared they would starve to death in their underground tomb.[2]

Mario recounts the day the "nightmare" began. Around lunchtime on August 5, 2010 the men gathered in a twenty-foot high cavern to catch the transport that would take them to the surface to eat their lunch. Had it not happened at lunchtime when they gathered together, many would have been scattered throughout the mine and would certainly have perished. Because Mario had on earphones, he didn't hear the mine rumbling, but he did see dust and debris. Then one of the miners came running through the dust and haze shouting "Cave in!!"[3] While some of the younger men cried and screamed, Mario searched for an escape route by walking around the subterranean tunnel system. He finally found a shaft with a ladder and started climbing, even though the walls were soft and rocks fell in his face, cutting his mouth, causing bleeding. Mario, thinking of his wife and children and how he didn't want his kids (ages eighteen and thirteen) to grow up without him, kept going. The ladder, which had not been maintained, ran out halfway up the two foot wide shaft, and though he tried to keep going without the ladder, when he saw two big rocks blocking the shaft, he knew there was no way out. Calling that discovery a moment of "utter despair," he came back down and reported it to the rest of the group.[4]

Once the men realized they were trapped, they formulated

a plan to keep their living area clean and patrol for signs of rescue attempts. They even set up a system of democratic government with each miner getting one vote in a majority-rule legal system.

Mario said he felt it was important that they stay busy and keep believing they would be rescued. He did everything he knew how to do to encourage the younger men and keep up their morale. Fifty-year-old Yonni Barios told reporters that Mario provided the true leadership in the darkest hours. "It was he who did everything for us, who organized the team. He encouraged us not to lose hope, that some day we were going to get out."[5]

Despite meager rations for the first seventeen days (two bites of canned tuna and a few sips of tainted water per day), Mario kept spirits from sinking by cracking jokes. He saw God's provision all around – from the water available to them in the industrial-sized drums to the timing of the cave in.

Although Mario cried often, he would not let the others see him, removing himself from the group before he allowed the tears to roll, "for the sake of morale."

Conditions in the mine worsened, from the sweltering heat (92 degrees F) to the dust filled air, causing eyes to burn and lungs to heave. Batteries in helmets died, resulting in fewer options to provide light in the darkness, and hunger began to take its toll.

Mario continued to encourage the younger miners. On about day ten, the mood was especially somber. Mario wanted to lighten it. He lay down on his makeshift bed and said, "Hey guys. I need to say something."

As the men gathered around, Mario pretended to be dying, and said very slowly, "My friends, say to my family that I love them. Tell them the money is in the ...." and then he let his head slump right before conveying the crucial information. As an aura of silence descended on the cavern, Mario held his breath. When he could hold it no more, he burst out laughing. Although some of the men yelled at him, many told him that it was the moment when they realized God had a plan for them, and even if they died, they would do it as a group and with dignity.[6]

Once the note that the men were well reached the surface, things took a turn for the better. Provisions were sent down – food, vitamins, medicines, rosaries from Pope Benedict XVI, and newspaper clippings about the rescue efforts and soccer games of note. Games, recorders, and Latin American music accompanied the food and water down into the mine, and, at the request of the miners, a book on public speaking. (Might as well develop some new skills that could be needed after the rescue).[7]

News from their families brought joy. On September 14, Ariel Ticona learned that his wife had delivered a healthy baby girl. All the miners joined in Ticona's celebration, especially when they learned the baby's name would be Hope, because, said his wife, those at Camp Hope above and the miners below would never lose hope for all the miners' safe return.[8]

As the trapped miners waited, the oldest among them,

sixty three year old Mario Gomez, became the spiritual leader of the group, setting up a makeshift chapel and leading the group in daily prayers. With the help of psychologists above, he counseled the men who needed help to continue going on. After the drill bit broke through and those above were able to get provisions and news to the miners, they could join together in prayers for their families and experts from around the world working to free them from the blocked mine.

Daily, the thirty three men joined together to pray for deliverance. Meanwhile, above ground, families of the miners at Camp Hope prayed for the safe return of their loved ones. As with any group, some were more spiritual than others. When the first miner, thirty one year old Florencio Avalos, the second in command, emerged from the dark, underground cavern to greet President Pinera and media from around the world, he knelt down and thanked God. After his wife hugged and kissed him, she threw a shawl with a picture of the Virgin Mary around his shoulders.

Because the world's attention was focused on the miners, prayers for their safe return went up from virtually every nation on earth. As believers put themselves in the shoes of the trapped men and sought to pray effectively, prayers for hope, health, patience, stamina and peace sustained those below. Prayers for wisdom, knowledge, skill, proper equipment, encouragement and success aided the rescue effort above.

Indeed, when the last of the thirty three miners emerged

from the cylindrical capsule sent through one half mile of rock and dirt to bring them up on October 13, 2010, sixty nine days after the cave in, every person on earth following the story knew he or she had witnessed a miracle.

As Mario Sepulveda shared, helping the other miners and focusing on their morale helped him. Keeping up his good humor and cracking his corny jokes made things seem normal to the others, even though at times he cried himself. Mario's mission below gave him a purpose and sustained him, but he continued to pray throughout the whole ordeal.

One of the great prayer principles is the prayer of agreement. Matthew 18:19 says, "Again, I truly tell you that if two of you on earth agree about anything they ask for, it will be done for them by my father in heaven." Many miracles have been documented after a church or community gathers together to pray for a person or situation for which there is no known or human solution.

When one of the teenagers at our church fell head first off a snowboard on a Boy Scout trip near Asheville, North Carolina and went into a coma on January 30, 2010, doctors gave his parents no hope for a full recovery. If he lived, they said, he'd likely be in a vegetative state and need full-time care for the rest of his life.

The youth leader at the church called a prayer meeting, inviting the community (especially his friends, classmates and fellow Boy Scouts) to join in praying for the impossible – his complete recovery. As we lit candles and joined in guided prayer for his recovery, his medical team, his parents and brother, we had a sense of God's presence with us. We wrote him notes, even though he was unconscious at the time, and presented them to his mother after the service (his father stayed at the hospital with him).

Nine days after the accident, on February 8, 2011 he woke up. The doctors at the stroke and neuro-science wing in the hospital where he was being treated were amazed.[9] One of them told his parents, "He shocked us all." Even these highly trained scientists knew they had witnessed a miracle – the miracle of prayers of agreement, just as the world stood in awe when the last of the thirty three miners emerged from the underground cave on October 13, 2010.

Chapter Sixteen

The Perpetual Caregiver
Creating a top ten list to deal with adversity

When Lou Brown Jewell's mother was diagnosed with ALS disease at age 70, Lou saw first-hand its ravages, as her mother, paralyzed from the waist up, lost the ability to eat. Her mom had always wanted to be size 8 (from size 16) and got there, but not in the way she would have chosen. As Lou watched her mom die, she had the distinct feeling her mother was teaching her how to die. "She never complained," Lou said. "In fact, she looked for the good in every circumstance. She kept a positive attitude through it all."[1]

As our nation celebrated its 200th anniversary, Lou found she had another problem – her twenty year old son's addiction to drugs and alcohol. She and her husband (president of a company listed on the New York Stock Exchange) sent him to rehab, but when he got out, he went right back to his old behavior patterns. Riding drunk on his bike one day, he was hit by a car and broke his arm. Lou, exasperated, told him he couldn't live at home until he quit using drugs and alcohol. He left and went to live with an uncle.

For a few years the pattern continued. Lou would get calls in the middle of the night saying her son was in jail, having been hauled in by the police for DUI. Then, one day, her worst fears were realized. He got behind the wheel of his car drunk and plowed into another vehicle, seriously injuring the woman in the other car and killing himself.

Lou leaned hard on her husband, two daughters, community of faith and Bible study friends. She also took comfort in knowing her son, whom she described as a "troubled soul" (manic depressive and schizophrenic) was at last free. "I was devastated, of course, but also relieved that we wouldn't be getting phone calls in the middle of the night any more. Now we could have peace."

After a breather of a few years, Lou encountered her next dragon – her husband was diagnosed with Parkinson's disease at age sixty. Four years later he developed dementia. As his condition worsened, Lou hired round–the–clock caregivers to keep him at home.

Lou herself went to a counselor, the chaplain at the hospital where her husband was being treated. She also found a Parkinson's disease support group, which met at one of the group members' homes. The group shared ideas and information and had lunch once a month. "The members of my group were incredibly helpful," says Lou. "We learned from each other and if one member was having a bad day, we could rally around him or her and share how we coped on our worst days."

Lou's husband's Parkinson's disease was one of the most rapidly progressing forms of the disease. When she lost him, she realized she had gained many new friends at the hospital where he had been treated and in her Parkinson's disease support group. She vowed to find a way to pay back all they had given her. She found it big time. She contacted the Emory University School of Medicine and met with leaders there over a period of time resulting in the establishment of a chair in neurology, named for her late husband. She also donated a significant amount of money to renovate the Parkinson's disease clinical research unit at a local senior care facility.

"To know the wonderful, vibrant person he was and to see how this disease robbed him of that was devastating," says Lou. "My husband was a very smart and capable man and he lost his sense of reasoning. He always had a booming voice but, over time, the timbre of his voice went down and he didn't talk at all."[2]

As Lou continued to recover from the loss of her husband, she told herself not to ask why. Instead, said Lou, ask *Why not?* "Who am I to think that I'm so special that nothing bad should touch me?" says Lou. "Job never blamed God for all his problems, even though his wife wanted him to," she noted, referring to the Old Testament prophet.

Lou looked for ways to help others as her broken heart was mending. A friend at church lost his wife after a prolonged illness, and she shared the name of the counselor who had helped her so much. To her surprise, the friend sent her a Valentine on Valentine's Day and later asked her out to dinner. They dated for several months and then Tom, her church friend, popped the question. Lou and Tom married in their seventies and looked forward to several great years together. By the time Tom reached his eighties, however, serious problems began to surface. He had trouble remembering things, and became confused about where he was. Medical tests revealed that he had Alzheimer's disease. Here we go again, thought Lou. She tried for a while to care for Tom at home, but the disease became progressively worse. Finally, in desperation, she realized she was going to have to put him somewhere he could be watched 24/7.

Lou researched all the available options carefully and finally selected one that provided individualized care for each Alzheimer's patient. "It broke my heart to put him there. I cried for two whole days. Now, here I am, still married, but living as a single person," she said.

As Lou continued to find help for others in their difficulties, she made a major contribution to her church to provide counseling for those who couldn't afford it themselves. Through the fund she established, many have found professional help to deal with problems surrounding addiction, illnesses, relationships, and financial loss.

I knew Lou well when I saw down to interview her. I had studied spiritual gifts and could easily identify Lou's – the gift of giving. I can't think of a cause this big–hearted woman doesn't give to. She has been recognized community wide for her generosity, and, in fact, in the fall of 2013 received the Philanthropist of the Year award for the Atlanta, Georgia area. While it was obvious to me that giving to others helped her heal, I wondered what else she might share that kept her ministering in the midst of her own grief. Her brown eyes sparkled and her petite frame, dressed in a smart navy and white pants suit, leaned forward as she told me there were ten things and shared her very own *"Top Ten Ways I have Dealt with Adversity in my Life"*:

1. <u>Make a list of everything for which you are</u> <u>thankful.</u> This was particularly helpful to Lou when her son died. She listed everything in his life for which she was thankful. I couldn't help but think of Philippians 4:8, "Finally, brothers, whatever is true, whatever is noble, whatever is right, whatever is pure, whatever is lovely, whatever is admirable – if anything is excellent or praiseworthy – think about such things."

   I remember reading a story once told by a Christian counselor who was working with a couple having marital difficulties and contemplating divorce. He asked them what attracted each of them to the other to begin with. They thought back and shared the qualities that led them into the marriage relationship. "Now," said the counselor, "I want each of you to go home and start a list of what you like about each other. Begin with these qualities and add to your list every day. Your homework is to bring it back to me at our next session."

The couple went home and worked on their assignments. The next time they met, the counselor took the lists and read them out loud and then discussed the positive character traits in each the other had listed.

The counselor told them to go home and continue working on the lists. After a few sessions of adding to their lists and discussing these qualities with the counselor, the couple informed him they didn't need to come back. "We're framing these lists and hanging them over our bed," the husband said. "Thank you for helping me see what a wonderful woman I married. Why would I want a divorce?" The wife nodded in agreement.

Or, what about the man who decided he wanted to sell his home to buy a better one? His real estate agent asked him to write up a description of the home she could put in the classified ad section of the paper (this was back in the days before online advertising took over). The man complied, listing all the positive qualities of the home. Of course he was anxious to verify his ad in the paper and eagerly turned to the classified ads section the day it first appeared. As he read the ad, the truth hit him – he was living in the home he had always wanted. He immediately called the agent and withdrew the listing.

2. <u>Pray.</u> Lou found peace and comfort by praying. Prayer is such a gigantic subject and there are so many kinds of prayer, perhaps the real question is "How do we pray when bad things happen?" Even then, I think it depends on what kind of bad thing has happened. We would pray differently if we lost a loved one than if we had just been diagnosed with a terminal illness. Regardless of our mountain of difficulty, prayer can have two very powerful effects on us: a) It keeps us focused on God, not the loss or problem. "You will keep in perfect peace those whose minds are steadfast because they trust in you", writes the Prophet Isaiah (Isaiah 26:3); and b) it changes our perception of the situation.

There's a famous picture used to illustrate how critical perception is. The picture, viewed one way, is a young, attractive, fashionable woman wearing the latest outfit. Viewed another way, an old lady with a prominent nose and thin drawn mouth appears. Same picture, different perceptions.[3]

Through prayer, we can apply Philippians 4:8, discussed above, to our problem.

3. <u>Surround yourself with positive friends.</u> This is when we need our friends who see the glass as half full, our "balcony people" as someone put it. We need cheerleaders, people who let us know they care about us and are in it with us. Then, we get a sense of being the one on the team who is carrying the baton and needs to finish strong for the team, not just ourselves.

When even one person is there – acting as cheerleader, coach or caring friend, we can turn our tragedies into triumphs. Examples would fill several volumes but one we all know is the Helen Keller story. Through her teacher, Anne Sullivan, who believed in Helen's intelligence despite her loss of sight and hearing, Helen became not only an inspiration for all hearing and vision–impaired persons but for every single one of us. Helen's education led her to write and speak to audiences around the world, raising the bar permanently for medically–challenged individuals.

4. <u>Do good deeds.</u> Lou put into effect the sowing and reaping principal. She sowed where she had reaped. She received help, strength, and

courage from neurologists, so she endowed a chair in neurology at the Emory University Medical School.

Her son had received counseling for his addiction problems and she herself went to counseling to recover from her losses, so she gave a significant gift to her church to provide counseling for those who couldn't afford it. She is currently discussing a major gift to aid research in Alzheimer's disease. Wherever Lou has taken out, she has put back in more. Her generosity does not stop there. She gives to any worthy cause that asks, after she checks out the ministry and is assured the funds would be well spent.

5. <u>Get in a support group.</u> Support groups help us to see we're not alone. Others suffer as we suffer. In fact, many people I know who have been in a support group say, "I thought it couldn't be any worse, but when I listened to some of the others in my support group, I realized some of them were worse off than I."

Support groups help us put things in perspective and give us input about how to cope with whatever it is we have to cope. Support group members often become friends for life, long after the group disbands.

6. <u>Find good scriptures and post them around the</u>

<u>house.</u> - Confessing scripture produces results. God says in Jeremiah 1:12 " ....You have seen correctly for I am watching to see that my word is fulfilled." Isaiah 55:11 says "So is my word that goes out from my mouth: it will not return to me empty, but will accomplish what I desire and achieve the purpose for which I sent it."

When we confess God's word into our situation, it produces fruit. If I am ill, I say, "By his wounds I am healed." Isaiah 53:4–5. Confession builds our faith, and faith moves mountains.[4]

7. <u>Don't isolate yourself.</u> Put in a positive way, lean on your friends. Tell them what you need, and let them help you. For some of us (I'm guilty big time of this myself), receiving help is hard, but I read something by Richard Foster that helped me to change my perspective (we need to do this sometimes). He called receiving help a ministry – the ministry of letting others serve us:

"It is an act of submission and service to allow others to serve us. It recognizes their "kingdom authority" over us. We graciously receive the service rendered, never feeling we must repay it. Those who, out of pride, refuse to be served, are failing to submit to the divinely appointed leadership in the kingdom of God."[5]

When we minister to others, we are blessed,

aren't we? So doesn't it make sense, when we are in need, they are blessed when they minister to us? Let's do our part to let the church be the church.

8. <u>Listen to soothing music.</u> We discussed music therapy in Chapter Ten. Good music heals, calms and soothes. It can minister to our souls in ways that words can't, stirring deep emotions within us.

9. <u>Make plans for something to which you can look forward.</u> It can be anything, Lou says – a movie, going out for dinner with a friend, perhaps a trip. This can actually serve two purposes: First it cheers us up. We may be down because of whatever mountain we're having to climb, and the thought of the pleasant event in the future makes us happy. Then, it can increase our faith, and faith moves mountains.[6] For example, suppose I'm going through a divorce and have used junk food as my "drug" of choice during my trying times. Now, I want to lose fifty pounds. If I buy two tickets (one for a friend) to the opera four months from now, I can buy a new dress today in the size I want to be then. The faith that I will be that size then works mightily in my favor.

10. <u>Maintain an attitude of gratitude.</u> If we can

train ourselves to be grateful for the "small" things in our lives, we simply won't have time to be depressed. Author Ann Voskamp accepted the challenge of a friend to list one thousand things for which she was grateful. The experience moved her so much she wound up writing *One Thousand Gifts, A Dare To Live Fully Right Where You Are*[7]. Ann noticed smells, sights, sounds, tastes and touches that brought her joy: rainbows in bubbles, the smell of freshly cut grass, the soft skin of a baby's cheek, the whispered 'thank you' of a friend she had helped, the taste of peppermint ice cream. If we're so busy being grateful, there's no room for fear. It's up to us. We can always determine how we react to the unwanted circumstances in our lives.

You've read Lou's list; now come up with your own. When you do, you'll have ten ways to cope with any curve ball coming over your home plate.

Chapter Seventeen

Living in a War Torn Country

Discovering the Power of Prayer

You can't blame a mother who objects to her daughter's engagement to someone who is of a different faith and already married to someone else. The suitor was determined, however, and madly in love. He obtained a divorce and promised his future mother-in-law to convert from Buddhism to Christianity. Only then was Chiang Kai-Shek able to obtain her consent and blessing to marry Mayling Soong, her daughter, better known as Madame Chiang Kai-Shek.

Mayling had been educated at Wellesley College in Wellesley, Massachusetts, receiving its highest academic distinction in her senior year. Following graduation, she returned to China to work, there meeting Chiang Kai- Shek, a rising star in the Chinese military. Ultimately he would become a Generalissimo, the leader of the Chinese Nationalist Party. In this role, he engaged in struggles with communist factions for his entire life, with Mayling at his side serving as translator, secretary, adviser and propagandist.[1]

Although Mayling's father was a Methodist Minister and her mother a devout woman of prayer, she was "merely a nominal Christian." Her mother spent hours communing with God, praying for the problems her children brought to her, followed with devotions of thanksgiving when the prayers were answered. "By experience we learned she could pray us through anything," wrote Mayling.[2]

But maternal prayer support came to an abrupt halt when Mayling's mother died, in 1931. She was devastated. No longer was her mother there to pray her through the personal as well as national crises. In desperation, Mayling began to pray with her husband who, faithful to his promise, had converted to Christianity. They prayed every morning together at 6:30 a.m. and every evening before retiring. Mayling writes, "...[A] deeper meaning has come of our prayers together. Many a time a feeling of spiritual peace seems to exude from within me, bringing completely annihilated self, with the mind in quiet and continuous absorption in the keen contemplation of God. When in this state, one is practically oblivious to the calls of this world, likes and dislikes, honor and fame, hate and love."[3]

Chaing Kai Shek had risen to power in a bloody coup

against the communists in 1927, where he led the Nationalist Party. In 1936, the Generalissimo was taken captive by some of his officers who were secretly in league with the communists and held incommunicado for days. The habit of daily prayer sustained him through this ordeal, writes Mayling.[4] It was Mayling who finally was able to negotiate his release, itself a miracle and answer to prayer.

The following year, as China fought Japan in the second Sino-Japanese war, the Chinese people were forced to set up a new capitol, Chungking, in the Szechuan Province, 1400 miles from the coast. Perhaps the greatest migration in history occurred as the Chinese people followed the Old Silk Route to their new home in the Szechuan Province. As they trekked to Chungking with their livestock, arsenals, and machines, using every method of transportation available, Mayling again turned to prayer. The Japanese invaders were making life miserable for the Chinese people.

For the first few years, bombers came by day and moonlight in "seemingly never ending waves of death." Mayling and the Generalissimo lived in underground shelters almost as much as they lived above ground. The shelters were damp and sweated with water dripping from sides of the cave, filled with the stench of dead air.

Mayling passed the time in the dugout by practicing her conversational French with a kind-hearted Belgian Priest, Father Weitz. One day when they had been in the dugout most of the day, Mayling suggested they go outside. After a while, the emergency alert sounded, and her husband called her to return to the bomb shelter. Just as they got to the shelter passageway, "the bowels of the earth seemed to be torn asunder" from the explosion of the bomb near where she and Father Weitz had been sitting. The French grammar book she'd been studying was sliced clear through with a piece of shrapnel. An apparent invisible shield had protected Mayling and Father Weitz from death as the bomb destroyed everything behind them.[5]

Some days the raids were so close and numerous no one had time to prepare food. Hours were wasted in the dugout – hours needed for work and rest. Tiredness permeated every fiber of the Chinese people's beings. Though the Chinese were determined not to cave in to the intense pressure being put on them by the Japanese, Mayling writes "determination and willpower are quite different from the power that comes from faith and prayer."[6]

About the third year of living half underground and half above ground, Mayling came to a point of spiritual desolation. Her prayers seemed empty – just words. She realized she was being poisoned by resentment, hated and bitterness toward the aggressors. She knew the teaching of Christ: love your enemies, pray for those who despitefully use you, but she couldn't do it.

As she meditated on her situation, words her mother had once spoken to her surged through her mind, " 'Vengeance is mine. I shall repay, says the Lord'. It certainly isn't yours." She had asked her mother to pray for the destruction of Japan, and her mother refused, reminding Mayling that what was God's prerogative was God's alone.

With her mother's reminder pounding through her mind, Mayling was able to unload her hate at the foot of the cross. For the first time since the bombings began, she turned the enemy over to the mercy and justice of God, and peace flooded her soul. She felt free.[7]

In 1943, Mayling was in the United States and made a speech at Madison Square Gardens, New York City. She told the audience:

> "There must be no bitterness in the reconstructed world. No matter what we have undergone and suffered, we must try to forgive those who injured us and remember only the lesson gained thereby. The teachings of Christ radiate ideas for the elevation of souls and intellectual capacities far above common passions of hate and degradation. He taught us to help our less fortunate fellow beings, to work and strive for their betterment without ever deceiving ourselves and others by pretending that tragedy and ugliness do not exist. He taught us to hate the evil in men, but not men themselves."[8]

For Mayling to speak those words and mean them with her whole heart, she had had to wrestle bitterness and hatred toward the Japanese, but these feelings had finally surrendered to a wider and deeper inner joy than she had ever experienced before.

Mayling came to see that all human suffering has a

purpose with God, leading to maturity and fulfillment. The quintessential example of suffering, the Prophet Job, emerged from his ordeal understanding God in a whole new dimension. As his time of suffering came to an end he confessed, "I had heard about you before, but now I have seen you..."[9]

When God asked Job to pray for the friends who had condemned and judged him, claiming his suffering was the result of some sin in his life, Job did not resist. When he prayed for his friends, the Lord restored his wealth and happiness. In fact, the Lord gave him twice as much as before.[10]

Mayling's struggles were not over. After Japan was defeated in World War II, the communists began a program of infiltration and smear tactics in China which eventually forced Chiang Kai-Shek to "retire" from office. He did so with great misgivings, leaving Chungking and retreating to the Island of Formosa. Mayling, who had been in the United States with her sister, heard God speak to her in an audible voice saying "All is right." She knew it was time to leave the United States and rejoin her husband on Formosa.[11]

As she flew to Formosa to join him, Mayling thought of how hard they had both worked to achieve a happy, free, literate, prosperous, and united country. She herself had been instrumental in building schools, hospitals and orphanages, undergoing privations and living in conditions she had never before known. Clearly prayer had seen her through, but as she asked God why the communists had prevailed and what she could now do, a reality hit her. While she had been trying to live a Christian life and make some social and political contributions, she had not been working directly for and with God. She had been doing things according to her agenda, asking for His help and blessing on what she had decided to do. She had, in effect, been using God instead of letting Him use her. As she watched the Pacific waves beneath her, an idea formed: start a prayer group. *What?* She asked herself. *A prayer group? People will think I'm a religious fanatic, overly zealous, self-righteous, pious.* Immediately the enemy began his attack.[12]

On stops over to Formosa, she was deeply moved at seeing all the Chinese people at the air fields to welcome her, the symbol of their beloved ancestral land. Young and old alike, cub scouts and grandmothers, were there to encourage her in the fight for a free China.

True to what she believed she had heard on the way to Formosa, when she was settled, she invited five devout Christian friends to join her in a weekly prayer group, standing on Christ's promise in Matthew 18:19 that if two agree on earth, whatever they requested would be done by their Father in heaven.

The group began with some hesitancy on the part of its members, as they took turns leading it. Some had never prayed out loud before. Beginning with silent prayer and hymns, the leader would share a testimony and then they would discuss it. The members then requested prayers for persons or situations. They would kneel and pray as the Spirit led.

In time the group grew into forty regular attendees, and they had to split into sub groups, meeting jointly every three months. Even nonbelievers were joining and coming to Christ in the process.[13]

Mayling began to experience the true difference in working in her own strength, asking for God's blessing, and working for and with God, asking Him to use her as his instrument. As God so often does, he asked her to do what she felt least qualified to do – start a prayer group. We see again the truth of the Apostle Paul's words, "My strength is made perfect in weakness."[14]

Mayling writes, "None of us can do much for ourselves. Men are spiritually powerful either through the work of the devil or the Holy Spirit. Purity of heart is found in both the intellectual and the lowly. God finds his own tools anywhere and everywhere."[15]

Members of the group bonded, and Mayling began to feel love for God. She'd always believed in God but now she began to see him as a loving Father, who was intimately concerned with her personal problems. She picked up the Bible and read the story of the crucifixion. When she came to the part where the soldier pierced the side of Christ, causing blood and water to flow from the wound, she began to weep. For the first time, she saw the suffering and pain of Christ were for her, and a sense of her own unworthiness overwhelmed her.

The prayer groups were all reporting miraculous answers to their prayers: A gambler joined one of the prayer groups and lost the urge for the excitement of the gambler's life; a morphine addict, unable to cure himself of the habit, joined a group and decided then and there with God's help he would stop using morphine; an adolescent boy, "going wild" keeping bad company, turned around and became a loving, loyal son.

As the prayer groups continued, Mayling and her prayer partners felt they should begin evangelical work among the armed forces. They put chaplains in one of the military hospitals and later in the army, supported by the tithing of the prayer group members. Eventually, eleven full-time chaplains were placed in the hospitals to do bedside visiting and hold regular Christian services. Grateful letters poured in from soldiers and hospital authorities. Before the chaplains came, officers and men would often commit suicide upon arrival at the hospital. In the hospitals where the chaplains were placed, not one suicide was reported.[16]

The successes, notes Mayling were not without disillusionment and disappointment. "Anyone who has tried to spread His word knows the impediments, the sharp rocks that lie on the path...time and time again the work has been obstructed, as though by the devil himself. But we persisted. The results are heartening."[17]

In moments of disillusionment and disappointment, Mayling remembered how small and trifling individual human disappointments were compared to the infinite love of God. Even Jesus frequently slipped away from the multitude to commune with his Father by himself and with his disciples. If He, the Son of God, needed to recharge His

189

spirit by prayer, how much more do we? Run to the arms of the One who longs to pour His blessings and strength into you. We are always at our best on our knees.

Chapter Eighteen

Loss of Family, Health and Wealth

Blind Faith in the Goodness of God

*T*he Old Testament prophet, Job, is the quintessential example of undeserved suffering. Job lived a model life - worshipping regularly, honest with all, and providing for the widows and orphans of his community.

On one surreal day, out of the clear blue sky, four separate messengers appeared to report the worst news imaginable: the Sabeans had murdered all but one of his field hands and had stolen his donkeys and oxen; lightning had struck his sheep and shepherds and had killed all but one lonely shepherd; the Chaldeans had raided his camels and had massacred all but one of the camel drivers; a tornado had hit the house where his seven sons and three daughters were dining, killing them instantly.

How did Job respond to this tsunami of bad news? He "got up and tore his robe and shaved his head. Then he fell to the ground in worship and said: 'Naked I came from my mother's womb and naked I will depart. The Lord gave and the Lord has taken away. May the name of the Lord be praised.'"[1]

We stand in awe and ask, "Job, are you for real? You didn't scream, 'Why, God, why?' You didn't tell God, 'That's it. I've had it with you?'" No, Job simply acknowledged that all his blessings came from God, and that what God gives, He may take away.

The story continues. Though Job lost his wealth and his children, he still had his health and his wife, until, that is, he was struck with painful, oozing ulcers from head to foot. His wife advised him to curse God, but, Job, instead, credited God with all the good in his life, "Shall we accept good from God and not trouble?"[2]

There's more to the story. Job's misery continues when three friends, hearing of all his misfortunes, appear to "console" him. Job pours out his heart, "What I feared has come upon me; what I dreaded has happened to me. I have no peace, no quietness. I have no rest, but only turmoil."[3] The friends proceeded to diagnose Job's problems and tell him what he needed to do. In a nutshell, they said, either Job had sinned or his children had sinned (and, by the way, noted the friends, the sin must have been horrendous to warrant the punishment doled out). Job needed to confess and seek forgiveness.

Job resisted the quick fix counsel of his friends, but they dug in deeper with more of the same sickening, spiritual bromide. Frustrated, Job cried out to God for an explanation. Whether or not an answer came, Job was going to stand on his faith in the goodness of God, "Though He slay me, yet will I hope in him."[4]

Finally, God speaks "from the eye of a violent storm." He recounts for Job His creation, showing Job divine mysteries too great for human minds. Job's journey, even though the valley of intense suffering, brings Job into the presence of God and to a place where he can hear and discern what he'd never heard before. Job stood amazed when he listened and encountered God directly, "My ears had heard of you but now my eyes have seen you."[5]

After God deals with Job, he turns to the friends, telling them they have not been honest with Him or about Him. They are instructed to offer sacrifices and then ask Job to pray for them, which they do. After Job intercedes for his friends, God restores Job's health, wealth, and family, blessing him with seven more sons and three beautiful daughters.[6]

Although Job trusts God through his suffering, he does not explain suffering. Suffering remains a mystery. We still ask, "Why do bad things happen to good people?" And still, we have no answer. But in the course of facing, questioning, and respecting suffering, Job encounters an even larger mystery - the mystery of God. "Perhaps the greatest mystery in suffering is how it can bring a person into the presence of

God in a state of worship, full of wonder, love and praise."[7]

Job exercised what I like to call "blind faith" - faith in God without seeing the answers or knowing the outcome.

Blind faith is faith that God knows best and the courage to leave the result totally and completely up to Him. It is trusting that the will of God is always good and the belief that God desires ever greater growth, expansion and multiplication for us. It is the conviction that God will give us that which draws us closer to Him for our ultimate joy and good. God always gives the best to those who leave the result to Him. That's blind faith.

Why should we trust God with the result? It's risky because we don't know the outcome. Let me offer three reasons.

1) <u>The character of God</u>. If God gave His only son for us, will He not freely give us all good things? The Bible tells us He will.[8]

   Warren Buffet's son had some money to invest. He gave it to his father and said "You invest it any way you want to, Dad." That was a no-brainer, we say. To give money to the most brilliant investor of our time with no strings attached is the only appropriate way to ask Buffet for help. It would be foolish to try to tell Warren Buffet how to invest. It's even more foolish to tell God, who knows more about everything than all of human kind collectively, what is best for us.

2) <u>Our own limited viewpoint</u>. We are handicapped. We see things only from our own limited perspective, which is often biased. We are bound by our human bodies, limited to one time and one space. We don't see the big picture, either for our own lives or for the lives of others. God does. He and He alone knows what is ultimately right and best for each of us and for the whole of us.

Ruth Bell Graham says before she met Billy, she asked God to let her marry several of the men she had dated. Only in His goodness and greater vision, she says, did God keep her on hold until the right one appeared.

3) <u>There is great good beyond what we can perceive through our five senses and we don't know how to ask for it</u>.

Putting the matter in God's hands opens the door for Him to give us good beyond what we know to ask. God has options we can't even imagine. Regrettably, we are usually only willing to utilize blind faith when everything else has failed.

Lynn Ratigan Smith represents her town of Newnan, GA in the Georgia Legislature. She has a long history of public service as a community leader. In the fall of 2001, the Speaker of the House asked Lynn to give the devotional. Lynn shared a story from her past about a difficult time in her life when she was searching for balance and God's guidance.

"One fall morning," she began, "I was feeling strangely and bizarrely ill. I had trouble breathing. Fortunately, about that time, my mother stopped by and insisted we go to the hospital. I was aggressively treated for anaphylactic shock and blood poisoning. I was then diagnosed with ulcerative colitis, an autoimmune disease that attacks the colon, an extremely painful and devastating disease."

"The degree of disease was so sudden and severe that modern medicine could not reverse it. I quickly lost my hair and wasted away to nothing. I was surviving on daily blood transfusions and hypoalimentation. My system started shutting down. I went back to the hospital, and the doctors and nurses went to work on me, but I could feel my life slipping away. I felt like I was drowning. I couldn't breathe. I desperately wanted to get away from what was happening to me. I pleaded, I bargained, I argued with God, but I kept getting weaker. I heard voices around me, but it was like I wasn't there. I was above it all, looking down on the people working on me. I knew then that I was dying – pleading, asking God, 'What do you want me to do? You know I need to be here for my family.' But then, as in a last moment, I felt a strange calmness. I realized what my prayer should be. It was the hardest thing I have ever done in my life."

"Finally, I prayed, 'God, not my will, but thy will be done.'"

"I survived that crises and another one three weeks later that was just as severe...I pray each day to take what I do seriously, but not take myself seriously."

And Lynn does. In leaving the decision to God, she found healing. Since then, she has served on many important committees in the House, including Appropriations, Natural Resources and Environment, State Planning and Community Affairs, and Civil Justice Reform Study Committee (tort reform).[9] And, God left her to be with her family as she requested.

The Power of Surrender

We usually think of surrender as defeat. The losing general surrenders to the winning general and submits to the terms the victorious side demands to end the war.

Yet, when we surrender to God's will, we actually place ourselves in a position of great strength. It's like Warren Buffet's son surrendering his money to his father with instructions, "You invest it any way you want." That son knew his father loved him and knew more about investing money than probably anyone in the world. To completely surrender it with no strings attached was the smartest, strongest action he could take with respect to his financial future. If his father invested brilliantly for everyone else, surely he would do at least as well for his own son.

Ruth Peale tells of desperately needing to find strength at a critical point in her life. She and Dr. Peal had returned home late one Sunday afternoon to find a message on their answering machine to call a surgeon at the North Carolina University Hospital in Chapel Hill.

When they called, the surgeon told them their son, John,

had come into the hospital in great pain. After testing, he continued, they had diagnosed an inflamed gallbladder. They were trying to reduce the infection and bring down his temperature so that they could operate.

Dr. and Mrs. Peale began praying for their son. At 11:15 that night, the surgeon called again with distressing news, "John hasn't responded to medication. The situation is becoming very serious. It's dangerous to operate under these conditions, but it's more dangerous not to. So I must operate."

Ruth told the surgeon, "Doctor, he is in your hands and in God's hands. Dr. Peale and I will be with you in prayer. Bring him through for us."

The doctor promised to do everything he could and call back in two or three hours, the time he thought the surgery would take.

John, their only son, was in great danger. "But, all our lives we have practiced, to the best of our ability, the idea of letting go and letting God. It is very hard to let go of your own son when everything within you draws him to yourself, but I believe we achieved it."

Four hours passed – no call. Then five, then six. Dr. and Mrs. Peale were on their knees. Finally, about 3:30 in the morning, they had (simultaneously) a strong feeling that John was all right and they cold leave him in God's hands.

At 6:00 a.m., the doctor called with good news, "John came through successfully. He's a very sick boy, but he is also a good, healthy boy...I feel he will be all right."

Later they learned that at about 3:00 a.m., the situation had become so serious that the hospital's chief surgeon had been brought in to take part in the operation. "Not in years have I had so great a sense of the goodness and love of God as I did that night," said Ruth.[10]

My husband and I had an experience with the prayer of surrender when our daughter was applying to college. The college of choice had wait listed her and we learned there were over one hundred people on the list for what would probably turn out to be only four or five places.

We set to work. We prayed. We got every alum we knew from that college to write. We recruited high school teachers to write (sometimes for the second time). We even managed a letter from one of our U. S. Senators. Finally, to cap it off, my husband and I drove five hours to the Admissions Office and (with as much humility as we could muster) told the people what a wonderful school they had and how much we hoped our daughter could go there.

Then, the difficult part began. We waited. It was very hard. Day after day and no response. One week, two weeks, three weeks. My husband was beside himself with worry. He lost sleep. His stomach hurt. He went to see his doctor to get help.

I had decided after about a week of praying for her to get in that one college, to surrender the situation to God, but he hadn't. He wanted his daughter at that school and he was holding out. Finally, I got a call from him at work. "I can't deal with this any longer," he said. "I'm surrendering this situation to God. Let His will be done."

"Thank goodness," I said to myself, "Now we can move on with our lives."

Forty-five minutes later my husband called again. "I don't believe this," he said. "The Admissions Office just called. They've accepted her." I cried (and so did he).

God was just waiting on a father to surrender his child's future so He could work a miracle and serve up a great big blessing.

Does it always work this way? We surrender and then we get what we want? No. But I believe it always works for the ultimate good of all concerned (including us). And it frees God to give us His very best, better than what we know to ask.

Jesus prayed the prayer of surrender in the Garden of Gethsemane. "My Father, if it is possible, may this cup be taken from me. Yet not as I will, but as you will."[11]

In fact, Matthew tells us that Jesus prayed this same prayer three times that night, each time leaving to the Father the best result.

What if Jesus hadn't done that? What if he had exercised His rights, called legions of angels down to fight for Him, killing all the Roman guards so no one was left to execute Him? He could have. He said so.[12]

But He didn't. He exercised blind faith in the goodness of God, trusting even though He knew the horrific pain that lay ahead. He believed God would bring a good that was greater than the pain. He believed something so wonderful would happen that His suffering would be more than worth it. Whatever would have happened to us had He not done so?

Isaiah prophesies: "Yet it was the Lord's will to crush him and cause him to suffer, and though the Lord makes his life an offering for sin, he will see his offspring and prolong his days, and the will of the Lord will prosper in his hand. After he suffered, he will see the light of life and be satisfied; by his knowledge, my righteous servant will justify many, and he will bear their iniquities...."[13]

Detachment

Once we pray the prayer of surrender, we must detach ourselves from the outcome. Detachment is the absence of a need to hold on to a person or material object. It actually brings us a sense of peace and great freedom as now the possibilities are unlimited and the burden has been cast on God. We are no longer bound; we are no longer responsible.

The prayer of surrender and detachment from the outcome are especially important if our prayer involves another person. There is a big difference between having a worthwhile personal goal for ourselves and having a goal for someone else (like wanting our child to marry a particular person). When our goal or prayer involves another person, we must be very careful not to manipulate.

Jesus was the most detached person ever to live. He was detached from everything (except His Father): money, peoples' opinions, the past, power, and his body and bodily comforts (just to name a few of the things he could take or leave). He turned everything over to God and taught us to do the same. He sought first the kingdom of God and His righteousness and everything He needed for his life here on earth was provided.[14]

Receptivity

Once we place our faith in God and surrender to His best, detaching ourselves from any one particular outcome, we must be receptive to what does come, even when we don't like it. Remember, it's for our ultimate good.

Do we like, after all, the pain or burn of pumping iron at the gym or the pain of recuperation from life saving surgery? No, we don't. But we know both are for our physical well being and the pain has to be endured to get us there.

To become receptive, we must first remove obstacles to receptivity. Among these are negative imaginations, mechanical reactions and frozen attitudes.[15] In the spiritual realm most of us like to fantasize and think of ourselves as wise and good. But we'd probably all admit we're not completely wise and good, and, in reality, most of us aren't nearly as wise and good as we'd like to imagine. If we've surrendered to God, He wants us to grow spiritually. We may have to change to do so. We have to be receptive. It may involve some emotional pain and giving up some cherished beliefs.

The search committee of a prestigious and wealthy Church had turned its search for a new senior pastor over to God. They met for prayer. They put together a list of criteria for which they were looking. They traveled all over the United States listening to pastors to find the man to whom they would extend their invitation. After all, they would be able to top almost any other church's salary. And they could offer many fringe benefits.

They compared notes. They debated. No one seemed exactly right for the job. Finally, they decided to ask the head of their denomination's regional office for help and advice. George, one of the search committee members, went to him and said, "We've been all over the country and can't seem to find the right man to fill our pulpit. Do you have any suggestions?"

"Why, yes," said the denominational official. "One of the best preachers in our denomination is right here in Atlanta. Her name is Joanna Adams."

George was hesitant. On the list of criteria compiled by the committee was: "No women."

He returned to the search committee to report. But before he could say anything, another member of the committee spoke, "Someone sent me a tape of a sermon by a pastor here in Atlanta and asked me to listen to it. I did and was blown away. I know we have "No women" on our list of criteria, but I think we should reconsider after hearing this tape by Joanna Adams," she said. Another member added, "I know Joanna Adams. She's terrific."

George was flabbergasted. He told the group of his conversation with the denominational official.

The committee was silent. Finally someone spoke. "Well,

we turned this search over to God. If He's telling us to call Joanna Adams, we'd better change our criteria."

The group agreed. After the entire committee went to hear Rev. Adams preach, they knew she was the right one for the job, and they extended the call.

Joanna accepted, and was a much beloved pastor there for several years, ministering to some of the most influential citizens in the community.[16]

Giving up our egos, our wills, our fixed beliefs, and our attachments to the only One who is forever wise and good is hard. But putting our faith in Him works all of the time for the good of all. What are we waiting for? As Mother Teresa prayed, "God, get me out of the way."

Endnotes

Chapter One - A Bullet in the Brain and a Trip to Hell

1. Chapter based on personal interview with Matthew and Nancy Botsford, July 16, 2013 (their real names), at their home on St. Simons Island, GA.
2. Nancy Botsford, *A Day in Hell, Death to Life to Hope* (OK: Tate Publishing & Enterprises, 2010), p. 17.
3. Id., p. 22.
4. Id., p. 28.
5. Id., p. 35-36.
6. Id., p. 38-39.
7. Id., p. 31.
8. Id., p. 76-79.
9. Id., p. 86.
10. Id., p. 111.
11. Zechariah 4:6.
12. See endnote 2.
13. Botsford, p. 147.

Chapter Two - Surviving a "Terminal" Illness

1. Chapter based on telephone interview February 5, 2013 with Georgia Shaffer (her real name) and on Ms. Shaffer's book, *A Gift of Mourning Glories: Restoring Your Life After Loss* (MI: Servant Publications, 2000).
2. Charles E. Hummel, *The Tyranny of the Urgent* (IL: Intervarsity Press, 1967).
3. Catherine Marshall, *A Man Called Peter* (MI: Baker Publishing Company, 1951).
4. Richard Wurmbrand, *Tortured for Christ* (OK: Living sacrifice Book Company, 1967).
5. Bruce Wilkinson, *The Prayer of Jabez* (NY: Multomah Publishers (a division of Random House), 2009).

Chapter Three - Living With Constant Pain

1. *"Degenerative Discs,"* www.webmd.com, (April, 2013).

2. Chapter based on personal interview with Julia Carmichael (fictional names used to protect privacy) April 15, 2013.

3. Tim Hansel, *You Gotta Keep Dancin'* (IL: David C. Cook Publishing Company, 1985) 34.

4. Luke 10:38-42.

5. Dan Grubbs, *"Dangerously Busy: Learming from Mary and Martha,"* http://www.sermoncentral.com/sermons/dangerously-busy-learning-from-mary-and-martha-dan-grubbs-sermon-on-discipleship

6. Sarah Young, *Jesus Calling* (TN: Integrity Publishers, 2004), 301.

7. Philippians 44:12-13.

Chapter Four - Loss of an Eye

1. Chapter based on personal interview with Victoria Underwood (fictional names used to protect privacy) January 30, 2011.

2. II Corinthians 12:9-10.

Chapter Five - The Agony of Physical Abuse

1. Chapters based on personal interviews with residents of the shelter sponsored by The Womens' Resource Center to End Domestic Violence, DeKalb County, GA, 2011-2013 (fictional names used to protect privacy).

Chapter Six - Coping with Ovarian and Breast Cancer

1. *"Fighting Back,"* http://www.dekalbmedical.com (Fall, 2007).

2. Chapter based on personal interview with Blackie

Scott Neese (her real name), 2012.

3. Kathleen Doheny, *"Have Purpose in Life? You Might Live Longer,"* Health Day Reporter, June 16, 2009, http://news.health.com/2009/06/16/have-purpose-you-might-live-longer/

4. Matthew 18:19.

5. Larry Dossey, *Prayer is Good Medicine* (NY: Harper Collins, 1996).

6. Id., p. 29-30.

7. Id., p. 31-32.

8. Id., p. 34.

Chapter Seven - A Missing Child

1. Chapter based on personal interview with Celia and Ben Summers (fictional names used to protect privacy) April 4, 2012.

2. Pat Schwiebert and Chuck DeKlyen, *Tear Soup* (OR: Grief Watch, 1999).

3. Anna McCraken and Mary Semel, *A Broken Heart Still Beats: If Your Child Dies* (MN: Hazelden, 1998).

Chapter Eight - Surviving emotional Abuse

1. University of Illinois of Urbana-Champaign, Il, Counseling Center: Emotional Abuse, http://www.counselingcenter.illinois.edu, citing Beverly Engle, The Emotionally Abused Woman: overcoming Destructive patterns and Reclaiming Yourself (NY: Fawcett Columbine, 1992), 10.

2. Id.

3. Id.

4. Id.

5. Chapter summarized and paraphrased from story told by Marilyn Honz (her real name) in her book,

Shame Lifter, Replacing Your Fears and Tears with Forgiveness, Truth and Hope (IL.: Tyndale House Publishers, Inc., 2009).

Chapter Nine - Forgiving a Murderer

1. Chapter based on personal interview with Reverend Pat Dunbar (her real name) May 21, 2013.

2. *"Crime and Capital Punishment,"* http://www.cncpunishment.com/forums/showthread.php?2972-Kevin_D-Foster-Death-Row (October 21, 2010).

3. Pat Dunbar, *"In the Court of Public Opinion,"* http://barefootprchr.org/2011/04/in-the-court-of-public-opinion/ (April 27, 2011).

4. Pat Dunbar, *"Oh, My Knocking Knees,"* http://barefootprchr.org/2012/06-oh-my-knocking-knees-sermon-62412/ (June 24, 2012).

5. Richard Foster, *Celebration of Discipline* (CA: Harper Collins, 1978), 5-6.

Chapter Ten - Contemplating Suicide

1. Chapter based on personal interview with Collin McPherson (fictional names used to protect privacy), 2012.

2. Frank E. Peretti, *This Present Darkness* (IL: Crossway Books, 1986, 2003).

3. C. S. Lewis, *The Screwtape Letters* (NY: Harper Collins Publisher, 1942).

4. I Samuel 16:23,

5. Amitra Cotrell, *"What is Healing Music?"* http://healingmusic.org/main/what-is-healing.htm (December, 2000).

6. Music therapy is being used in critical care units of hospitals to help patients heal more quickly through

relaxation and accepting the condition and treatment without excessive anxiety, reports Dr. Raymond Bahr, director of coronary care at St. Agnes Hospital in Baltimore, MD.

7. Joel 2:25.

Chapter Eleven - Parenting Down Syndrome Children

1. Chapter based on personal interview with Emily Kincaid (fictional names used to protect privacy), 2011.

2. Psalms 91:14-16.

3. Psalms 108:12-13.

4. Kelle Hampton's (her real name) story is summarized and paraphrased from her web site, www.kellehampton.com

5. Philippians 4:8.

Chapter Twelve - Dealing with Loneliness and Disabilities

1. Phyllis Hobe, *Angels in Disguise* (NY: Guideposts, 2009), 169-172.

2. John Grogan, *Marley and Me* (NY: Harper Collins, 2005).

3. http://www.servicedogsforamerica.org

4. Id., Testimonials.

5. Valverde Martina, *"Boy Suffering from Autism Gets Service Dog, Thanks to Large Donations,"* KFOX 14 News, http://www.Kfoxtv.com/news/el-paso-boy-who-suffers-autism-gets-service-dog-do/NSLSg/ (September 25,2012).

6. http://www.servicedogsforamerica.org/testimonials

7. Story based on personal interview with Pat and Don

(last name withheld to protect privacy), 2011.

8. http://pegasusridingacdemy.com/index. php?option=com

9. Karen Winegar and Judy Olausen, *Saved Animals and the Lives They Transform* (PA: Da Capo Press, 2008).

10. Story based on personal interview with Terry and Karen (last name withheld to protect privacy), 2012.

Chapter Thirteen - Confronting Challenge and Controversy

1. 163 U.S. 537 (1896).

2. 347 U.S. 483 (1954).

3. *"Civil Rights: The Little Rock School Integration Crisis,"* Eisenhower Museum, www.eisenhower. archives.gov/research/online_documents/civil_rights_ little_rock.html

4. *"Martin Luther,"* English Bible History, www.greatsite.com/timeline=english-bible-history/ martin-luther.html

5. Chapter based on personal interview with Sarah Mitchell Parsons (her real name), 2010.

6. Sarah Mitchell Parsons, *From Southern Wrongs to Civil Rights,* (AL: The University of Alabama Press, 2000), p.xxv.

7. Id., p. 12.

8. Id., p. 17.

9. Id., p. 19.

10. Id., p. 21.

11. Id., p. 25.

12. Id., p. 27.

13. Id., p. 32.

14. Id., p. 33.

15. Id., p. 35.

16. Galatians 3:26, 28.

17. Parsons, p. 57.

18. Id., p. 60.

19. Id., p. 63.

20. Id., p. 78.

21. Id., p. 79.

22. Id., p. 89.

23. Id., p. 94.

24. Id., p. 116.

25. Amos 5:24.

Chapter Fourteen - Financial Distress

1. Gary Keesee, *Fixing the Money Thing* (PA: Destiny Image Publishers Inc., 2011), p. 97.

2. Proverbs 22:7.

3. Psalms 37:21.

4. Exodus 23:30.

5. Malachi 3:10.

6. Malachi 3:8-9.

7. Malachi 3:10.

8. I Kings 17:7-16.

9. Adam Grant, *Give and Take* (NY: Penguin Group, 2013).

Chapter Fifteen - Trapped Underground for 69 Days

1. Joshua Buck, *"Nasa Team Honored for Assisting chilean Minor Rescue,"* http://www.nasa.gov/home/hqnews/2011/sep/Hq11-302_Sammies.html (Sept. 2011).

2. Caroline Graham, *"Mail Online - The Amazing First Interview with One of the Chilean Miners,"* http://www.dailymail.co.uk/news/article_1321230/ chilean-miners-world-exclusive-interview-Mario-Sepulveda.html (October 21, 2010).

3. Id.

4. Id.

5. Id.

6. Id.

7. Id.

8. Elliott McLauglin, *"Down Below Chilean Found Hope in Family, The Little Things,"* CNN World (October 11, 2012).

9. Mary J. Loftis, *"Crash Course,"* The Emory Magazine (Spring, 2011).

Chapter Sixteen - The Perpetual Caregiver

1. Chapter based on personal interview with Lou Brown Jewell (her real name) August 11, 2011 and follow up 2013.

2. Jennifer Johnson, *"Emory Health Center Newsletter,"* February 10, 2009.

3. Eric W. Weisstein, *"Young Girl-Old Woman Illusion,"* Mathworld - a Wolfram Web Resource, http://mathworld.wolfram.com/younggirl-oldwomanillusion.html

4. Matthew 21:21.

5. Richard Foster, *Celebration of Discipline* (NY: Harper Collins, 1978,1988,1998), p. 136-137.

6. Matthew 21:21.

7. Ann Voskamp, *One Thousand Gifts: A Dare to Live Fully Right Where You Are* (MI: Zondervan, 2010).

Chapter Seventeen - Living in a War Torn Country

1. Wolf Murr, *"Madame Chaing Kai-Shek,"* www.wellesly.edu/Anniversary/Chiang.html (August 14, 2000).

2. Madame Chaing Kai-Shek, *The Sure Victory* (NJ: Fleming H Revel Co., 1955), p. 9.

3. Id., p 12.

4. Id., p. 13.

5. Id., P. 16.

6. Id., p. 18.

7. Id., p. 19.

8. Id.

9. Job 42:5.

10. Job 42:12-17.

11. Madame Chaing Kai-Shek, p. 23.

12. Id., p. 27.

13. Id., p. 31.

14. II Corinthians 12:19.

15. Madame Chaing Kai-Shek, p. 32.

16. Id., p. 41.

17. Id.

Chapter Eighteen - Loss of Family, Health and Wealth

1. Job 1:13-21.

2. Job 2:10.

3. Job 3:24-26.

4. Job 13:13, 19.

5. Job 42:1-6.

6. Job 42:12-17.

7. Eugene Peterson, *The Message* (CO: Navpress, 1993), p. 718.

8. Romans 8:32.

9. Mary Ben Christiansen, *"Women Leaders in the State of Georgia,"* presented May 14, 2004 to the Wednesday Morning Study Club, Atlanta, GA. (paper on file at the Atlanta History Center).

10. Norman Vincent Peale, *The Positive Power of Jesus Christ* (NY: Guideposts, 1980).

11. Matthew 26:39.

12. Matthew 26:53.

13. Isaiah 53:10 & 11.

14. Matthew 6:33.

15. Vernon Howard, *The Power of Your Supermind* (NY: Prentice Hall, 1975), p. 33.

16. Story based on interview with George (name changed for privacy reasons).

Afterword

You have just read eighteen stories of people who found strength from God to endure and even move to a higher level of wisdom, compassion, and creativity through their trauma. All of us go through storms. If you would like the presence and protection of God, the Father, in the midst of your personal situation, whatever it is, and have never known how to receive it, you can do that very simply right now.

The Bible tells us we come to the Father through Jesus, his Son. Receiving Jesus, all He is and all He did for us, is as simple as asking Him to come in to your life and take over. He is ready, willing and able to exchange His righteousness for your sin, His peace for your turmoil, and His blessings for your trash. Just pray this prayer:

"Dear Jesus,

I haven't known you, but I want to. I believe that you died on the cross for me, and ask you to forgive me for everything wrong I have ever done. Please come into my heart and take over. Give me your desires for my life and guide me in all that I do. You are my God and my King from this point forward. Thank you that I have eternal life through you in heaven. Amen."

If you prayed this prayer for the first time, please find a good church and tell the pastor what you have done.